Favourite
Irish Names
for
Your Baby

Favourite Irish Names for Your Baby

FROM AARON TO ÚNA

LAURENCE FLANAGAN

GILL & MACMILLAN

Gill & Macmillan
Hume Avenue, Park West, Dublin 12
with associated companies throughout the world
www.gillmacmillanbooks.ie

© Laurence Flanagan 1993, 2013
978 07171 5619 1

Printed in Malaysia

A CIP catalogue record for this book is available from the
British Library.

1 3 5 4 2

Eibhlín a Rún
To Eileen

(and to Fraoileann)

GUIDANCE FOR USERS

A name printed thus: **ABBÁN** is an Irish form of a native Irish name.

A name printed thus: *AILIS* is an Irish form of a borrowed or imported name.

A name printed thus: AIDAN is an English form or equivalent of an Irish name.

NOTE: No suggestion about the pronunciation of Irish names is given, because of the dialectal differences in the pronunciation of such common names as *Seán*, *Gráinne* and *Deirdre*; it is instead suggested that the advice of a local speaker of Irish be obtained.

TABLE OF CONTENTS

There are often several different spellings of Irish names. The Table of Contents lists most variable spellings of most names. Thus Áedán, Aodhán and Aidan are listed separately in the Contents, although they are all covered by a single entry in the text.

Page references in bold type show that the entry indicated is a substantive one.

INTRODUCTION

As a result of a study of Irish personal names (i.e. fore-names, including Christian names) included in a master-work compiled by M.A. O'Brien, *Corpus Genealogiarum Hiberniae*, it was calculated that there then existed some 3,500 examples of significantly different Irish personal names, up to a date of around 1100 A.D. In all, these names were shared by some 12,000 persons. About 4,000 people, however, shared 100 of the names, leaving the remaining 3,400 names to be shared by fewer than 8,000 persons. Out of the 3,500 names included, a mere 102 are women's names. There exists, however, a supplementary source — a prose text, based on a twelfth-century poem on famous women by an historically-minded poet from Co. Fermanagh — which increases the number of women's names to just over 300.

From the names listed in the *Corpus* a 'League Table' of the first four male names can be drawn up:

Áed:	250 instances
Eochaid:	220 instances
Cormac:	100 instances
Domnall:	100 instances

As far as women's names are concerned, from the prose text, a 'League Table' for the first five places reads as follows:

Sadb:	25 instances
Cacht:	23 instances
Eithne:	20 instances
Mór:	18 instances
Gormlaith:	16 instances
Órlaith:	16 instances

These samples are, of course, static: they show, at first sight, no indications of changes in taste, though a run-through of names appearing, year by year, in any of the annals, suggests that changes in taste do exist — a phenomenon that is attested by the speed with which borrowed or imported names, whether borrowed from the Vikings, such as Goffraid, or from the Anglo-Normans, such as Rémann, were adopted by the Irish.

At one time, any similar statistical survey of Irish names, or name-forms, would have entailed an enormous amount of drudgery, extracting the raw-material from the registrars of births. Fortunately, the Central Statistics Office of Ireland, taking advantage of the fact that modern records have been computerised, began to compile an annual list, showing the frequency with which each name used appeared. The results were surprising in many ways. Apart from the fact that English names took the lead by a wide margin (Jack, with 914 instances, was by far the most popular boy's name, while Sophie, with 599, was the most popular name for girls) the number of Irish names that scored highly was impressive. From the latest available list compiled, for the year 2010, a league table for the 'Top 25' names, the top five Irish boys' names reads as follows:

Sean/Seán:	812 instances
Conor/Conchobar:	714 instances
Ryan/Rían:	662 instances
Michael/Micheál:	455 instances
Cian:	417 instances

For the top five names for girls we have:

Aoife:	419 instances
Ciara:	361 instances
Saoirse:	353 instances
Caoimhe:	316 instances
Niamh/Niam:	286 instances

The contrast between 2010 and 1100 is fairly stark: none of the Corpus names appears in the 2010 lists. In addition, any survey of Irish fore-names demonstrates the extent to which borrowed names, with an Irish form, have been thoroughly 'naturalised'. Thus Seán, Liam, Éamonn, Eoin, Colm, Sinéad, Róisín, Eileen, Caitlín and Siobhán.

For the purposes of this book, to these have been added some 50 other names used for children derived from the lists of births appearing in Irish newspapers. The other 30-odd have been added mostly on the grounds that they are possessed by people known to myself, or because, in a few instances, they seem to be names that enjoy a modern, usable form, and deserve, therefore, to be reinstated in contemporary usage.

The stories or extracts of stories attached to the names (except in those fairly few instances where no stories appear to exist, or where the name has been of such recent coinage as not to have a suitable, necessarily deceased, owner) have been chosen to cover as deep a span and as wide a spectrum of Irish life and culture as possible, covering Mythology, History, Hagiography, Music, Politics, Art and even Archaeology.

ABBÁN, ABÁN *m*

With the meaning of 'little abbot' it was the name of a St Abbán
mac ua Cormaic, said to have been baptised by St Iobhar (though
it is unlikely that the Ibhor of Beggerin Island was the Ibhor
involved), who was his uncle and associated with a church at
Magharnaidhe, which has been identified with Adamstown,
Co. Wexford. He also established a church named Cill Abbáin.
His Feast Day is March 16th; the English form is simply *Abban*.

ADOMNÁN, ADHAMHÁN *m*

Meaning 'the timorous one' this was the name of one of the
most famous abbots of Iona and the biographer of Colmcille.
He was born near Raphoe, Co. Donegal, in 624, and seems to
have entered the local monastery founded by Colmcille before
going to Iona to continue his studies. He returned to Ireland and
while here was instrumental in securing the release of sixty
captives taken in Meath by Saxon raiders. He arranged a meeting
with King Aldfrith to negotiate their release; when Adomnán
and his companions hauled their ships onto the shore Adomnán
drew a circle round them and the place where the ships lay
immediately became an island. The Saxons took note and took
the negotiations so seriously that Adomnán quickly achieved
his two objectives — the release of the captives and an imme-
diate cessation of the raids. He returned to Iona in 678 where,
becoming Abbot in 679, he remained until his death in 704.
He is said to have had a knowledge of Greek and Hebrew as
well, of course, as being fluent in Latin. He is best known for his
Vita Sancti Columbae (Life of Saint Columba). He is Patron of the
Diocese of Raphoe; his Feast Day is September 23rd. The
received English form of his name is *Eunan*.

ÁED, AODH *m*

Is the word *áedh* (fire) and was one of the most common names
in early Ireland and borne by a score or so of early saints,
including Áedh mac Bricc of Rahugh, Co. Westmeath, whose

oratory on Slieve League, Co. Donegal is still a place of pilgrimage on November 10th every year. It was also the name of at least four Uí Néill High Kings, including Áedh Allán, who, in 737, joined Cathal, King of Munster for a *Ríg dal* (royal conference), at Terryglass, Co. Tipperary, a celebrated Leinster monastery on Munster soil. Oddly enough Terryglass was the abbey of which a most celebrated Áedh was abbot. Known as 'lector of the High King of the Southern half of Ireland' Áed Cruamthainn, between 1151 and 1224, compiled there, at the behest of Bishop Finn of Leinster, the book known as *The Book of Leinster*, but more accurately as *Leabhar na Núachongbhála* (The Book of Noughavel, from the Tipperary monastery where it had been kept for so long). This compilation is said to 'sum up all the learning of the monastic period of Irish writing' and its compiler is described as the 'prime historian of Leinster in wisdom and knowledge and book-lore and science and learning'. Despite the fact that Áed is almost universally anglicised as H*ugh* it has no connection with this English name.

ÁEDAMMAIR, AODHAMAIR *f*
It is a derivative of the name *Áed*. It was the name of the first woman traditionally to have been 'given the veil' by St Patrick — her father, understandably, was called Áed. She established a nunnery at a place called Drom Dubhain, near Clogher, Co. Tyrone. Her Feast Day is February 18th. There is no received English form of the name.

ÁEDÁN, AODHÁN *m*
A diminutive form of *Áedh*. This name was in fairly widespread use in early Ireland, both among lay people and clerics — at least a score of saints bore the name. Probably the best-known is Aodhán of Ferns, Co. Wexford — who is actually better known by his 'pet' form, Maodhóg. His mother, Eithne, and father, Sedna, had been childless for some time and prayed often to God that they might have an heir. One night while they were

asleep a star fell from the heavens on each of them and soon afterwards a soothsayer said to Eithne: 'Woman, you have conceived a wonderful son, and he shall be full of God's Grace'. Eventually Aodhán went to Wales to study under St David; here he performed many miracles, including miraculously creating roads through bogs and healing the deaf, lame and blind son of a British king. When his education was completed he returned to Ireland and founded his monastery at Ferns. While the monastery was under construction his monks complained of the lack of water on the site: Aodhán instructed them to cut down a certain tree; instantly a spring of water gushed from its place. He died at Ferns between 625 and 632; his Feast Day is January 31st; *Aidan* is the normal English form.

ÁEDNAT, AODHNAIT *m*
A feminine diminutive form of Áed; there is a recorded St Áednat, whose Feast Day is November 10th, of whom nothing is known. Probably the best English form is *Enat*.

ÁEDUCÁN, AODHAGÁN *m*
A diminutive form of *Áedh*, which was quite common in medieval Ireland. One of its more renowned bearers was Aodhagán Ó Raithile, the last of the great Munster poets, born in Kerry in 1670. He saw the new planters as upstarts and boors, satirising their greed and ignorance. He lamented the demise of the old Gaelic order in lyrics (the so-called 'aisling', or 'vision' poetry) which addressed Ireland as a beautiful woman awaiting the return of her true lover from beyond the sea. He died, as he had lived, in poverty, and is buried at Muckross Abbey. The normal English version of the name is *Egan*.

ÁENGUS *see* ÓENGUS

AIDAN *see* ÁEDÁN

AIDIN *see* ÉTAÍN

AILBHE, AILBE *m & f*

The name is probably derived from the old root *albho* (white). One of the best known bearers of the name was Ailbhe Grúad-brecc (Ailbhe of the variegated — i.e. red and white — cheeks), who was rated third in the list of 'the four best women in Ireland that ever lay with a man' compiled, or at least cited, by Cailte, a warrior of the Fianna. She was a daughter of Cormac mac Airt and was one of the women who won the affection of Finn mac Cumall. It was also used as a male name, of whose bearers one of the most famous is St Ailbhe, of Emly, Co. Tipperary, who was a contemporary of St Patrick, having been consecrated a bishop in Rome. He was described as 'that other Patrick of the island of Ireland'. He died in 527; his Feast Day is September 12th. The male name has been anglicised as *Alby*; there is no received anglicised version of the female name.

AILEEN *see* EIBHLÍN

AILIS, ALIS *f*

A name borrowed from the Norman-French *Aliz* which was imported by the Franks into Ireland. The English equivalent is *Alice*.

ÁINE *f*

Meaning 'delight, pleasure, splendour', once used as a name for males in parts of the country, is now exclusively feminine. It is identified with the goddess of love and fertility, Áine, who was a daughter of Eogabail, foster-son of Manannán Mac Lir, the sea-god. She frequently became involved with humans in romantic contexts. One tale about her tells how she was raped by Ailill, a king of Munster; in revenge she cut off his ear before using her magic to bring about his death. She continued to be prominent in folk-lore, though in a rather less salacious role and her name is associated with many places throughout the country. In Teelin, in Co. Donegal, for example, there is a hill called Cnoc Áine, which was considered a dangerous place for young girls and with which a mysterious piper is associated; a discontented wife is said to have asked Áine of Cnoc Áine Áine Chnoc Áine,/Caidé lagaíos na fir?' (Áine of Cnoc Áine/What weakens men?). It was also the name of a married daughter of Diarmaid Mac Murchada, king of Leinster, who in 1169 was given to Richard Fitz Gilbert, Earl of Pembroke, as part of the deal by which Diarmaid obtained the Earl's assistance. The English names *Anne*, *Annie* or *Hannah*, of biblical derivation, have nothing in common with it and the English form is simply *Aine*, though presumably *Enya* is a rather aberrant form.

AISLING, AISLINN f
Meaning 'a dream, a vision' is one of the collection of Irish common nouns that have in recent times been pressed into service as personal names. Possibly its application to the type of patriotic/romantic poetry that developed as a nostalgic genre in which Ireland was addressed as a beautiful woman had a part in encouraging this transfer. Since, presumably, the sound of the name is part of its attraction there is no point in using an anglicised form.

ALBY *see* AILBHE

ALICE *see* AILIS

ANA *see* DANA

ANGUS *see* ÓENGUS

ANNE *see* ÁINE

ANNIE *see* EITHNE

ANTHONY *see* ANTOINE

ANTOINE

ANTOINE *m*

A name made popular by St Anthony of Padua, who died in 1231, and introduced to Ireland by the Franks. It never became very common in Ireland. One bearer of it was the blind Mayo-born poet Antoine Ó Reachtabhra, who wrote songs and ballads on events of the day — such as the success of Daniel O'Connell in the Clare by-election; he also wrote love-poetry and died in 1835. The English equivalent is, of course, *Anthony*.

AODH *see* ÁED

AOIBHEANN, AOIBHÍN *f*

Meaning 'fair form' or 'beautiful sheen', this was the name of the mother of St Enda of Aran and his sisters, St Fainche of Rossory, Co. Fermanagh, and Dáiríne. It was also the name of a number of princesses. It is usually anglicised *Eavan*.

AOIFE, AÍFE *f*

Meaning 'beautiful, radiant (goddess)' was very common among the heroines of early Irish legend. One of these was sister to the female warrior Scathach who instructed Cú Chulainn in the martial arts after he had been rejected as a suitor for Émer by her father Forgall. In the course of war between Scathach and Aoife, Cú Chulainn overcame Aoife by guile; she and her sister were reconciled. Aoife fell in love with Cú Chulainn and bore his child. Years later their son, by then a young warrior, was slain by Cú Chulainn who was unaware that he had slain his son by Aoife. Although it has been anglicised as *Eva* there is no real connection and the name is better left as *Aoife*.

ART *m*

Literally means 'a bear', but by extension is used in a figurative sense as 'champion'. One of the earliest and best-known people to carry it was the legendary Art Óenfer (Art the lonely), the father of Cormac mac Airt. Art's father, Conn Cétchathach (Conn of the hundred battles), had taken as a concubine a 'demoted' goddess called Becuma; she was jealous of Art and wanted to dispose of him, so she tricked him into going in quest of a beautiful maiden called Delbchaem. The whole point of sending him on this quest was that poor Art had to endure, and overcome, a series of dreadful dangers, including a giant and the dilemma of choosing between two cups, one of which contained a deadly poison. Finally he had to conquer Delbchaem's parents — Morgan, lord of the Land of Wonder, and his consort, a monstrous female warrior called Coinchind — before he could rescue Delbchaem from the tower in which she was imprisoned. Art successfully overcame all his obstacles, and, finding that Delbchaem (fair of form) lived up to her name, brought her home, and was able to banish the loathsome Becuma. This, however, is not the happy ending of a romantic tale; on his way to the battle in which his death was pre-ordained Art stopped overnight in the house of a smith and seduced his daughter Achtán; it was she who gave birth to his son Cormac mac Airt. The name has no connection with the English *Arthur* and is best used simply as *Art*, even in English contexts.

BÁIRBRE f

A borrowing of the feminine form of the Greek word βαρβαρος (savage, uncouth) after the highly popular medieval, but probably mythical, St Barbara. The English form is of course, *Barbara*.

BAIRRE *see* BARRFIND

BARBARA *see* BÁIRBRE

BARRA *see* BARRFIND

BARRFIND, BAIRRFHIONN *m & f*

Meaning 'fair-haired' or 'fair-headed' this was the name of several saints, one, at least, a female. One of the male saints of the name is Barrfhionn of Kilbarron, Co. Donegal (the place-name enshrines his personal name). He has been identified with the Barrfhionn who, himself, had voyaged to the 'Land of Promise of the Saints' and, by his description of his adventures, inspired Brendan of Clonfert to undertake his more renowned voyage. Pet-forms of the name in Irish are *Bairre*, *Barre* and *Barra*. *Barrin* would be an acceptable English form, while *Barry*, more common than the name itself, is the usual English version of the pet-forms.

BARRIN *see* BARRFIND

BARRY *see* BARRFIND *or* FINNBARR

BÉBINN, BÉFIND, BÉIBHINN, BÉBHIONN f

Meaning 'white or fair lady' it was a very popular name in early Ireland. One of the more bizarre stories about a bearer of this name is contained in the so-called *Colloquy of the Ancients*. Finn mac Cumall and Goll were sitting on a bank when they perceived a woman approaching them. 'By my word and indeed,' said Goll, 'never have either I or any other seen a woman bigger than

12

she.' She told them that she was Bébhionn, daughter of Treon, and that for the third time she had run away from her husband, Áedh son of Cedach. She explained that she had come to seek safeguard with Finn, which Finn and Goll mac Morna agreed to give. While they were drinking and listening to the harp that evening, in the course of which she let down her hair — 'in seven score tresses her fair curly golden hair, at the wealth of which when it was loosened all stood amazed' — they saw a tall young man coming towards them. 'If the girl was big, he was bigger still.' Bébhionn said: 'I know him; that is the man seeking to escape whom I come.' Then, before any of those present knew what was happening he thrust his spear clean through Bébhionn and passed on his way out through the crowd. They set off in pursuit, but failed to catch him before he escaped into a great galley. Poor Bébhionn's soul departed from her body and the place where she was buried was called *The ridge of the dead woman* after her. *Bevin* is an acceptable English form.

BERACH, BEARACH *m*

Means 'pointed' or 'sharp'; it was the name of several saints, such as St Berach, who had been Abbot of Bangor, Co. Down, as successor to St Ségán O'Cuinn, for a single year between Segan's death and his own. His Feast Day is April 21st. *Berach* seems a reasonable form in English.

BERRACH, BEARRACH *f*

Although included in the list of 'the four best women in Ireland that ever lay with a man', Berrach came only fourth. This was Berrach Brec (Freckled Berrach), daughter of Cás Cuailgne of Ulster and the wife of Finn mac Cumall (even here she managed only to come third!). Of the four, however, she excelled in goodness and generosity. Before becoming Fionn's wife she had been in fosterage with the parents of Goll mac Morna. Eventually it was agreed that she become Fionn's third wife; she went off with Fionn and bore him three sons, Fáelán, Áedh and Uillen. With the passage of time, however, the clanna Morna 'turned to be spoilers and outlaws', with a particular grudge against Fionn, and in three battles with the Fianna they came off worse. Then, at the instigation of Conán mael mac Morna, a 'breeder of quarrels among followers, a malicious mischief-maker in army and in host', they decided that anyone close to Fionn was fair game. They offered Berrach impunity if she forsook Fionn and brought with her all her jewels and valuables. Proudly she refused, so they surrounded the *dún* in which she was living and attacked it. She made to escape to her galley and on the very shore she was hit by a javelin 'full in her chest, in her very bosom'. There is no received English version of her name.

BEVIN *see* BÉBINN

BLANID *see* BLÁTHNAT

BLÁTHNAT, BLÁNAID, BLÁITHÍN f
Are diminutive forms of *blath* (flower). One Bláthnat was daughter of Mend and, rather against her will, wife of Cú Roí, a west Munster king and hero. She, moreover, had fallen in love with Cú Chulainn, Cú Roí's enemy. Cú Roí's fortress was cunningly constructed so that nobody could find its entrance; Bláthnat poured milk into a stream that ran through the fortress and Cú Chulainn, by observing where the milk-stained water emerged, was able to gain access to the fortress.

Cú Chulainn's attack was successful, Cú Roí was slain and Bláthnat went off in the arms of her lover. Cú Roí's bard, Ferchertne, however, survived the attack and lived to take his revenge on his king's betrayer. As Cú Chulainn and Bláthnat were making their way along the Beara peninsula they paused, while Bláthnat looked over some cliffs; Ferchertne leapt forward, seized Bláthnat by the waist and jumped to his death over the cliffs, carrying her with him. An English form, Blanid, is sometimes used.

BLINNE f

A modern — and local — form of Mo-Ninne (Moninna). Her original name appears to have been Darerca; she is said to have been baptised by St Patrick himself before establishing her first community, consisting of a widow with a child and eight virgins near her home at Faughart, Co. Louth. Here they remained for some time, until she found the social intercourse with her friends, neighbours and family too much of a distraction from her religious commitments. She and her nuns, therefore, decided to journey down to the extreme south of Ireland, to Beggerin Island in Co. Wexford where they lived under the rule of St Íbhar, a precursor of, and, until they were reconciled, a rival to, St Patrick. Her Feast Day is July 6th; the English form is simply Blinne.

BRÉNAINN, BREANDÁN m

It has been suggested that this may be a borrowing from the Welsh breenhin (prince) and that the modern form Breandán came back into Irish through the Latin Brendanus. The most celebrated bearer of the name is St Breandán of Clonfert, Co. Galway, who is thought to have been born near Tralee in Co. Kerry towards the end of the fifth century. Because of an expedition he undertook he is known as 'Breandán the navigator'. In the course of their seven-year voyage Breandán and his companions visited many fabulous lands and islands (one of the 'islands' on which they landed started moving — it was a whale) in the Atlantic (now identified as including Iceland, Greenland and, probably, America). His fantastic voyage is the subject of a classic medieval tale, Navigatio Sancti Brendani (The Voyage of Saint Brendan), which was translated into virtually every European language. He founded a monastery at Ardfert, Co. Kerry, and later one at Clonfert, Co. Galway, where the Archangel Michael visited him in the form of a bird and held a conversation with him. His death is recorded in 577; his Feast Day is May 16th. Among the other early saints who bore the name is St Breandán of Birr. The accepted form in English is Brendan.

BRIAN *m*

There is some doubt as to the origin of this name: one authority held that it was a borrowing from Breton, another that it developed from an earlier, disyllabic, Irish name B*rion*, in which case the meaning is 'noble or high'. By far the most eminent bearer of the name was Brian Boru, who, effectively, in the closing years of the tenth century and the opening years of the eleventh, achieved a degree of authority over the whole of Ireland, after the death by treachery of his brother Mathgamain. He first secured his position in Munster and then waited until he was clearly dominant throughout the southern half of Ireland. By 997 Brian's position was recognised by Máel Sechnaill, King of Tara and a meeting was convened at Clonfert at which it was agreed that the northern part of Ireland was Máel Sechnaill's, the southern part Brian's. After successfully putting down a revolt by the Leinstermen and their allies, the Norse of Dublin, Brian felt strong enough to turn his attention, at last, to the northern part of Ireland, until, in 1002, he received the submission of Máel Sechnaill; by 1011 he had achieved a sort of authority over the entire country by defeating the last independent peoples, the Cenél Conaill. His final action, by which, with the aid of the propaganda of *Cogadh Gaedhel re Gallaibh* (the war of the Irish with the Foreigners), he became a national Hero, was the Battle of Clontarf, on Good Friday, 1014, in which he himself was slain. The English form is, fortunately, exactly the same as the Irish.

BRIGIT, BRIGHID, BRÍD *f*

With the meaning 'High Goddess', Brigit was the pagan goddess of poetry. While several Christian saints shared the name, Brigit of Kildare is pre-eminent. She was born in the mid-fifth century, in Co. Kildare. From her childhood she displayed conspicuous generosity to the poor and earned an enormous reputation for tending the sick, especially lepers. Her great convent was at Kildare, on a piece of ground that was given her by the King of Leinster, marked by a large and conspicuous oak-tree — hence the name — 'The Church of the Oak-Tree'; this was to become the principal church of the Kingdom of Leinster. It was unusual for Irish monastic foundations in that it was a 'double' monastery, with both monks and nuns, and ruled over by an abbot-bishop and an abbess. Many 'Lives' of Brigit were written, some of them early, such as the *Bethu Brigte*, a ninth-century translation from an eighth-century Latin *Life*. Other later versions were written in Flemish, French and German. She was known as 'The Prophetess of Christ, the Queen of the South, the Mary of the Gael'. One of the most charming relics of her are the Brigit's Crosses, of rushes or straw, of different styles in different parts of the country. She died about 524 and there is a tradition that she is buried, along with Patrick and Colmcille, at Downpatrick, Co. Down. Her Feast Day is February 1st. While *Brigit* is a perfectly acceptable form, due to confusion with the Swedish St Brigitta, *Bridget* is often also used; Irish diminutives such as *Brídín*, *Brighdín* or *Bríde* are also popular.

BRÓGÁN, BRÓCCÁN *m*
There seems to be no agreement as to the meaning of this name. There are several saints who bore it. Perhaps one of the most interesting is the Brógán who was St Patrick's scribe during the saint's meeting with the Fianna, described in *The Colloquy of the Ancients*, to whom Patrick said from time to time, after a particularly wondrous tale told by Caeilte: 'By thee be written down all that Caeilte has uttered.' On hearing some music played by the minstrel Cascorach mac Cainchinne, thinking that St Patrick disapproved of it, Brógán remarked: 'If music there be in Heaven, why should there not on earth'? Apart from this sage interjection Brógán's recording of the tales is a fitting memorial to him. There is no need for a separate English form.

BRÓNACH *f*
It means 'sorrowful'. It was the name of St Brónach, of Kilbroney, Co. Down, about whom little is known, though her name is

enshrined in the place-name. Her crosier is preserved in the National Museum of Ireland and her bell in the Roman Catholic church in Rostrevor. Her Feast Day is April 2nd. There is no recognised English version of her name, but the spelling *Bronagh* seems to be favoured.

CÁELFIND, CAOILAINN f

A compound of the words *caol* (slender) and *fionn* (fair). It was borne by several Irish saints. Even of the best known of these, little certain is known: it seems she was, at least, a daughter of a descendant of Fergus, son of Ros, son of Rudraighe. Despite the uncertainty of her lineage, and of her birth-place, a hagiographer was able to say of her: 'This pious lady quickly won the esteem and affection of her sister nuns by her exactness to every duty, as also by her sweet temper, gentle, confiding disposition and unaffected piety.' Her Feast Day is February 3rd; the most usual English form is *Keelin*.

CAHÁN, CATHÁN m & f

This name is derived from *cath* (battle) and presumably means 'a battler'. The 'original' Cathán who gave his name to the O'Cahan (O'Kane) sept of Co. Derry is said to have been a son of Eoghan, and therefore a grandson of Niall of the Nine Hostages. Even among the O'Kanes the name is not frequently found as a forename, but one Cathán, son of Ruaidhrí, is recorded as dying in 1383. Another Ó Cahán is commemorated in the exquisite fifteenth-century tomb in Dungiven Priory; traditionally this is supposed to be the tomb of Cooey-na-Gall, who died in 1385. A scurrilous story is told of an eighteenth-century O'Cahan who was returning from a banquet in the house of a neighbouring chieftain. His horse never drank anything but wine, but, not having been offered any at the banquet, was mad with thirst. Some English soldiers at a check-point were regaling themselves from a hogshead of wine they had looted; as soon as the horse smelt his favoured beverage, he rushed headlong towards it and while he had his head immersed in the hogshead, his master's was struck off by the soldiers. As the name of a female it was borne by Cathán, abbess of Kildare who died in 854. *Cahan* would be an acceptable English form, or, like the surname, *Kane*.

CAHIR *see* **CATHÁIR**

CAIRELL, COIREALL *m*

No explanation appears to have been offered for the derivation of this name. It was borne by several saints including St Cairell of Tír Róis, who was with St Colman Elo when he founded his monastery at Lynally, Co. Westmeath. His festival is kept on June 13th, at Ballymacward, Co. Galway. The name could be anglicised as *Kerill* or even *Karel*.

CAIRENN, CAIREANN *f*

Is said to be a borrowing from the Latin *Carina*. The best known bearer of the name was Cairenn Chasdubh (Cairenn of the dark curly hair), the daughter of Scal Moen, king of the Saxons. She was the second wife of Eochaidh Muigmedón and the mother of Niall of the Nine Hostages. Eochaidh's first wife, Mongfhionn, resented and hated her, and forced her to do menial work even late in her pregnancy. She gave birth to Niall while engaged in such menial labour. Her name could be anglicised as *Karan* or even *Karen*.

CAITLÍN, CAITILÍN *f*

Is derived from from the old French form *Cateline*, for Catherine of Alexandria (who, sadly, herself, was the product of pious fiction). It was introduced to Ireland by the French-speaking Anglo-Normans. A Caitilín, daughter of Mac Sweeny and wife of O'Doherty, died in 1530, while a most moving tribute is accorded to Caitilín, daughter of Domnall and wife of Tadg, son of Cormac Óg, who died in 1592, describing her as 'a sensible, pious, charitable and truly honourable woman, after having gained the victory over the world, the Devil and the people'. In the eighteenth century among the terms used for Ireland, in nostalgia for the days of the old Irish aristocracy, was *Caitlín ni Houlihan*. The common and widespread anglicisation is, of course, *Kathleen*, which has entered English usage as a distinct name; *Cáit* is a common Irish diminutive form.

CAITRÍONA, CATRAOINE f

Is derived from the old French form, *Caterine*, also for Catherine of Alexandria. It, too, was brought to Ireland by the French-speaking Anglo-Normans, where it became popular, particularly among the medieval aristocracy. Several medieval churches in Ireland are dedicated to St Catherine, including St Catherine's in Dublin in 1219 and the Priory of St Catherine at Aughrim, Co. Galway, in about 1206. It was in common use in the later medieval period in Ireland. Cataríona, daughter of O'Duigenan, died in 1525 and was honourably buried in the monastery of Donegal. The Countess Cateríona was, naturally, one of those who accompanied Hugh, son of Ferdorcha, Earl O'Neill, when he boarded the ship in Lough Swilly, in 1507, that was to carry him and O'Donnel into exile, in an exodus that has been described: 'This was a distinguished crew for one ship; for it is indeed certain that the sea had not supported, and the winds had not wafted from Ireland, in modern times, a party of one ship who would have been more illustrious or noble, in point of genealogy, or more renowned for deeds, valour, prowess or high achievements.' *Tríona* is a common Irish diminutive while *Catriona* is an acceptable English alternative to *Catherine* or *Katherine*. The diminutive *Triona* is used as well in English.

CALBHACH m

Means 'bald'; it was a popular name among certain families, including the O'Donnells, in the later middle ages. One O'Donnell who bore the name was the eldest son of Manus O'Donnell. Possibly through jealousy of his half-brother, Hugh, he quarrelled with his father and tried to claim leadership of the clan. Indeed in 1548 he and his ally O'Cahan were defeated by Manus near Ballybofey. Father and son were summoned to Dublin in 1549 by the lord-deputy, because of the disorders their enmity was creating. Calbhach was granted the castle of Lifford, but fresh disturbances broke out until, in 1554, assisted by a large body of Scottish mercenaries, Calbhach overran

Tyrconnel, captured his own father and put him in confinement. His brother Hugh invoked the assistance of Shane O'Neill, but Calbhach took their forces by surprise and defeated them. He was in favour with the English government but in 1561, just as he was about to be dubbed Earl of Tyrconnel, he and his wife were captured by O'Neill; Calbhach was kept in close and secret confinement; his wife became O'Neill's mistress. Calbhach's durance was, indeed, vile: he was forced to wear an iron collar round his neck, fastened by a short chain to fetters round his ankles. He was eventually released, but failed to observe any of the conditions imposed. Going first to Dublin to seek redress, where he met scant sympathy, he went to London, direct to Elizabeth, who was more sympathetic, and ordered the lord-deputy to act on his behalf. A large force moved north under Sir Henry Sidney and restored Calbhach to power in Donegal, as an ultra-loyal subject of the Queen. He did not, however, live long to enjoy his restored honours. On October 26th 1566 he fell from his horse in a fit and was killed. *Calvagh* is the received English form.

CALVAGH *see* CALBHACH

CAOIMHE *f*
A name meaning 'beauty' or 'grace'; it is the name of a virgin saint from Killeavy, Co. Down, about whom virtually nothing else is known; her Feast Day is November 2nd. A possible English form would be *Keeva*.

CAOIMHÍN, CÁEMGEN *m*
A name meaning 'comely child' or 'beautiful birth' it seems to have been singularly appropriate for its most celebrated bearer, Caoimhín of Glendalough. He received his early training at Kilnamanagh, near Tallaght, in Co. Dublin. Here he showed early signs of his piety and purity: a young woman, obviously considering him comely indeed, was bent on enticing him

from his celibate life — she pursued him; he hid in a bed of nettles; she persisted; he retaliated by striking her with a bunch of nettles. So successful was this treatment that the young woman repented and lived the rest of her life in purity and sanctity. Caomhín took himself to a remote spot in the Wicklow Mountains, intent on living as a hermit: to his chagrin disciples flocked to him in such numbers that he had to move his church to a more spacious area on the eastern side of the Upper Lake, Glendalough. The monastery grew, both in numbers and in reputation, soon becoming a place of pilgrimage — a pilgrimage to Glendalough was considered the equivalent of one to Rome. It was Caoimhín's custom to remove himself to a tiny cell during Lent; one day he was kneeling in prayer, with his hand stretched through the little opening that served as a window; a blackbird flew onto it and eventually laid her egg in it; so patient, kind and gentle was he that he remained kneeling until the egg was hatched and the fledgling flown. Caoimhín died about 620; his Feast Day is June 3rd. The received anglicised version of his name is *Kevin*.

CAR(R)A *see* CERA

CAROLL *see* CERBALL

CATHAÍR, CATHAOIR *m*

One suggested, but not universally accepted, interpretation is 'battle-lord'. One bearer of the name was the truly legendary Cathaír Mar, ancestor of the Leinstermen, who is credited with the begetting of thirty-three sons and with reigning over Leinster for fifty years. More recently there was Sir Cahir O'Doherty who, having cast his lot in with the English, earned his knighthood on the field at Augher and was favourably received in London by Queen Elizabeth. He was made a justice of the peace and an alderman of the city of Derry. After the departure of O'Neill and O'Donnell from Lough Swilly in 1607 he was foreman of the jury which found the Earls guilty of treason. He himself was subsequently charged with treason by the governor of Derry, Sir George Paulet. In 1608 his quarrel with Paulet induced him to sack and burn Derry and kill Paulet. Inevitably retribution soon followed: a force was sent from Dublin against him and on 5th July, 1608, he was shot dead near Kilmacrenan. The best form of the name in English is *Cahir*.

CATHAL *m*

Means 'strong in battle'. It was the name of kings of both Munster and Connacht. A more recent bearer of the name, who was highly successful in living up to it, was Cathal Brugha, born in Dublin in 1874. He joined the Gaelic League in 1899 and in 1913 became a lieutenant in the Irish Volunteers. During the Rising of 1916 he was second-in-command at South Dublin Union, was severely wounded and, as a result, lame for the rest of his life. Despite this he played a leading role in the War of Independence, becoming Minister of Defence between 1919 and 1922. In the Civil War he fought on the Republican side and died, of wounds received, in 1922. Although it is commonly regarded as the equivalent of *Charles*, Cathal has no connection with this name; *Cathal* is the best form in Irish or English.

CATHERINE *see* CAITRÍONA

CATRIONA *see* CAITRÍONA

CEALLACH, CELLACH *m* & *f*

Is an old name with the meaning 'bright-headed'. There is an interesting instruction in the 'Rule' of St Máel Rúain of Tallaght that in the event of pre-natal baptism 'Either *Flann* or *Cellach* should be given as a name for they are both common to a male or a female.' In documentary sources it is more common as a male name, and a number of saints bore it, including

Ceallach of Killala, Co. Mayo, son of a king of Connacht, who led an involved and interesting life, torn between Church and State. Another Cellach, Cellach Cualand, was father of St Caíntigerna (Kentigerna) of Loch Lomond in Scotland. A son of Cormac mac Art, whose main contribution to legend or history is that he raped a relative of Aonghus 'of the terrible spear', was called Cellach. It was also borne by several Leinster rulers. An anglicised form, *Kellach*, has been used; possibly *Kelly* is more acceptable to modern taste.

CERA, CEARA f

One meaning suggested for this name is 'red' or 'bright red'. It was the name of one of the wives of Nemed, the legendary invader of Ireland, and was also the name of three saints, one of whom was St Cera of Killahear, Co. Monaghan. She was an associate of St Mac Cártan, of Clogher, Co. Tyrone, and of St Tigernach of Clones who consecrated a church for her and placed the deanery of Clones under her patronage. Her Feast Day is September 9th; her name is best anglicised as *Cara* or *Carra*.

CERBALL, CERBHALL m

This name means 'brave in fighting' or 'valorous in battle'. Cerball mac Muirecáin, king of Leinster, was one of the three kings that were married to Gormlaith, who had begun her marital career as wife of Cormac, the bishop-king of Cashel, who had slain her first husband before dying himself in an accident in 909. In the later Middle Ages it was a favourite name among the learned family of Ó Dálaigh (Daly). It is appropriate that this *ainm chine* (name in the family tradition) should have been borne by the fifth President of Ireland, who has been described as 'a lover of the arts and a linguist, a man of wide culture'. Having served for two sessions as Attorney General, and having been appointed Chief Justice in 1961 Cearbhall Ó Dálaigh was the agreed choice for President in 1974, of all political parties. He died in Dublin in 1978. A suitable English form is *Carroll*.

CIAN *m*

With the meaning of 'ancient' or 'enduring' it was the name of several legendary figures, including Cian, son of Ailill Olum, who gave his name, as ancestor, to the peoples known as Cianachta. Another Cian was a son of Dian Cecht, the physician and surgeon. On one occasion, seeking a stolen cow, he went to Balor's tower, where he encountered Ethlínn, Balor's daughter, who was kept imprisoned in the tower so that she would remain celibate. This was because of a prophecy that Balor would be slain by his own grand-child. Cian seduced Ethlínn and then went home with his cow. The name has been anglicised as *Kean*; perhaps *Kian* would be more suitable.

CIAR, CIARA *f*

Means 'dark' or 'black'; the best recorded bearer of this name is St Ciara of Kilkeary, Co. Tipperary. At the request of St Brendan of Clonfert she extinguished 'a pestiferous fire' by dint of her prayers. As the size of the community at the monastery she had established at Kilkeary increased she felt it necessary to establish another. She obtained a site for herself and her five companion nuns from St Fintan Munnu. She died in 679. Her Feast Day is January 5th (and October 16th); the best English form of her name could be *Kiera*.

CIARÁN *m*

Derived from *ciar* (black). There were a number of saints who bore this name, of whom the best known are Ciarán of Seir Kieran, Co. Offaly, known as 'Ciarán the Elder', who, after pursuing his studies in Europe, settled as a hermit in the Slieve Bloom Mountains, with no company other than the wild beasts; of these a wild boar is said to have helped Ciarán build his cell by cutting branches with his tusks. Disciples flocked to him, his monastery prospered and became the burial-place of the kings of Ossory, while Ciarán became the patron of the Kingdom of Munster. His Feast Day is March 5th. The other highly celebrated

Ciarán was, of course, Ciarán of Clonmacnoise, Co. Offaly — a monastery which he founded on February 25th, 547, only to die seven months later. His monastery grew in importance, eventually becoming a monastic city with twelve or thirteen churches or oratories, and an unrivalled centre of Irish art and literature. From its workshops came such masterpieces as the Cross of Cong and St Manchan's Shrine; from its scriptoria some of the most important Irish manuscripts such as *Leabhar na hUidre* (The Book of the Dun Cow) and *The Annals of Clonmacnoise*. His Feast Day is September 9th. The accepted anglicised form is *Kieran*.

CILLÉNE, CILLÍN, CILLIAN *m*

One suggested derivation is from *cill* (church). There were, understandably, several saints of this name. Of one of these, who went as a missionary to Artois in the seventh century, an amusing story is told. On arriving one day at the house of Count Eulfus he asked for a drink and was refused. When the count returned from a hunting trip he found that each and every cask of wine in his house was empty. He immediately realised the reason for this and, sending for Cillian, apologised. The wine returned forthwith to the casks. His Feast Day is November 13th; *Cillian* or *Kilian* are acceptable anglicised forms.

CILLIAN *see* CILLÉNE

CINÁED, CINÁETH, CIONAODH *m*

It is argued that this name is Pictish in origin and was borrowed into Old Irish. It was the name of the high king Cináed mac Irgalaig, who was slain at the battle of Druim-Corcain in 727. The Pictish connection is enhanced by the fact that in 775 in the course of internecine conflict among the Dal nAraidhe (Cruithne of Co. Antrim), Cináedh Cairgge, son of Cathasach, was slain; again, in 807 Cináedh, son of Conchobhar, was slain by the Cruithne. The Cruithne seemed to enjoy continuing internecine strife, for in 831 Cináedh, son of Echaid, king of the Dal nAraidhe of the North, was killed, through treachery, by his associates. Its non-Cruithne use, however, was demonstrated in 849 when Cináedh, son of Conaing, king of Cianachta, turned against Máelsechnaill, king of Ireland, and wasted the Úi-Néill 'from the Shannon to the sea', and destroyed Lagore, Co. Meath. He met his just reward in 850 when he was 'drowned in a pool' by Máelsechnaill and Tigernach 'with the approval of the men of Ireland, and of the successor of Patrick especially'. It was a name favoured too in Scotland: in 857 Cináedh mac Ailpín, king of the Picts, died. He is better known as Kenneth McAlpin and the normal English form of the name is *Kenneth*.

CLEENA *see* CLÍODHNA

CLÍODHNA, CLÍONA *f*
In Tir Tarrngaire (The Land of Promise) Manannán mac Lir had a poet called Libra, who had three beautiful daughters: Clíodhna, Aeife and Édaein — 'three treasures of spinsterhood and chastity; whom it was not to be feared that anything but the pernicious effects of continence would ever kill'. It happened, however, that on the one night all three fell in love: Aeife and Édaein with Lodan, the son of the king of India, and Eolus, the son of the king of Greece, and Clíodhna with Ciabhán, son of Eochaid of Ulster. The three girls arranged to elope with their suitors; the two foreign kings embarked in one currach with their women, Ciabhán and Clíodhna in another. Ciabhán landed and went off hunting game; a great wave came roaring in and drowned Clíodhna — and the wave at this point (identified as Glandore Harbour) was known as *Tonn Chlíodhna* (Clíodhna's Wave). An anglicised form, *Cleena*, does exist, but *Cliona* is also used as an English form.

CLÍONA *see* CLÍODHNA

CLODAGH *f*

This is the name of a river, *Clóideach*, a tributary of the Suir, in Co. Waterford. (There are other rivers, mainly, if not solely, in the southern counties, with the same name). It was bestowed as a name on the daughter of the Marquis of Waterford — in the best tradition of the Irish martyrologies, which are accused of 'making a saint out of a placename'. It is sometimes anglicised as *Cloda*, but *Clodagh* is used in English as well.

CÓILÍN *m*

A name derived from *Col*, the French diminutive of *Nicholas*, introduced by the Franks, or Anglo-Normans. It was the name of St Nicholas of Myra, in Asia Minor, but in the eleventh century his remains were moved to Bari, in southern Italy, and he is also therefore known as St Nicholas of Bari. Churches were dedicated to him in Galway, Adare and other places in Ireland; he is the saint who is now rendered as *Santa Claus*. The usual English form is *Colin*.

COLIN *see* COILÍN

COLM, COLUM, COLUMB *m & f*

A name derived from the Latin *Columba* (dove). While there are several Irish saints (male and female) of this name, Colm, who was to become known as Colmcille (Colm of the Church), is clearly the most famous and important. As well as founding a string of monasteries in Ireland, including such notable ones as Doire Cholm Cille, in 546, which was to become modern Londonderry, he founded others at Durrow, Co. Offaly; Kells, Co. Meath and Moone, Co. Kildare, before going to Iona intent on bringing Christianity to, or rather back to, the people of Scotland. His early studies were with the celebrated Finian of Movilla, in Co. Down. In his youth his Guardian Angel informed him that he was permitted to choose his virtues: Colm chose virginity and wisdom; as a reward for choosing the right ones he was also awarded the gift of prophecy. As proof that he put it into effect he did indeed prophesy:

> My Irish people are to me a cause of sorrow, since in time to come they will wage war on one another, will injure, hate and wickedly slay, will shed innocent blood.

His biography, *Vita Sancti Columbae* (The Life of Saint Columba) was written by his successor as Abbot of Iona, St Adomnán. He died at Iona in 597. His remains are said to have been transferred to Downpatrick, Co. Down, where they lie with those of Patrick and Brigit. His Feast Day is June 9th. *Colum* or *Columba* are the most usual English versions. In early days it was also used as a name for females, with at least one female saint.

COLMÁN *m*

A diminutive form of *Colm*. It was the name of several famous saints, including St Colmán Elo of Lynally, Co. Westmeath, St Colmán mac Léníne, of Cloyne, Co. Cork, St Colmán mac Duagh, of Kilmacduagh, Co. Galway as well as nearly 250 others. So common was it that on one occasion at Lismore, when work was being carried out in a river bed, and the supervisor called out for a monk called Colmán to do something, twelve monks of that name jumped fully clad into the river. There is an interesting story involving St Colmán Elo. He was asked the reason for the eight canonical hours; his reply was: 'Eight faults there be that cleave to body and soul of every man; now these eight hours purge them: Prime against immoderate gluttony; Tierce, against anger born of many causes; cheerful, lightsome Noon we constantly oppose to lust; Nones against covetousness so long as we are on the breast of weary Earth; pleasant and profitable Vespers we oppose to sore despair; Compline, against perverting weariness: this is a fair partition; cold Nocturns that equally divide the night, against inordinate boasting; Matins of God's atoning Son, against enslaving sullen pride'. There is no specific English equivalent, so *Colman* may be used in English as well as in Irish.

COMHGHALL, COMGAL *m*

With the meaning of 'fellow hostage' it was used by several saints, the most eminent of whom was St Comhghall of Bangor, Co. Down. His birth, between 515 and 520, had been predicted, first by St Patrick, some sixty years earlier, and, closer to the date, by St Mac Nisse of Connor, who observed on seeing his pregnant mother: 'That woman bears a King; he shall be adorned with all virtues and the world shall be illuminated with the lustre of his miracles.' He studied under St Fintan at Clonenagh, Co. Laois, before returning to the North of Ireland and founding his monastery at Bangor, in or about 555. The monastery flourished and at one time there were reputed to be 4,000 monks with the grace of God under the yoke of Comhghall at Bangor. It was known as 'The Vale of the Angels'. Bangor's greatest claim to fame, however, was as the centre whence so many Irish missionaries, including Columbanus of Luxeuil in France and Gall of St Gallen in Switzerland, set off to labour on the mainland of Europe. Comhghall died in 601 or 602 having been given the Last Rites by St Fiacre of distant Ullard, Co. Kilkenny, who after Comhghall's death took one of his arms back with him for enshrining. His Feast Day is May 10th; an acceptable English form of his name would be *Cowal*, which has the merit of indicating the approximate pronunciation.

CONALL *m*

Means 'as strong as a wolf'. It was borne by many people famous in legend, as well as by a number of saints. The most illustrious, in some ways (he gave his name to an Irish county), was Conall, one of two sons of Niall Naígiallach (of the nine hostages). He and his brother Eoghan gave their names to *Cinél Conaill* and *Cinél Eoghain*, which were to become *Tír Conaill* (Tirconnel = Donegal) and *Tír Eoghain* (Tyrone). Despite the fact that the two supreme septs descended from them (the O'Donnells and the O'Neills) were in constant conflict for nearly a millennium, the leaders of the two septs, the Earl O'Neill

31

and the Earl O'Donnell, with their wives and families, departed in the same ship from Lough Swilly in 1607. Either *Conall* or *Connell* are acceptable English forms.

CONÁN *m*

Means 'hound' or 'wolf'; it was the name of a member of Fionn's Fianna, Conán mac Mórna, unflatteringly described as 'the Fianna's man of scurrilous and abusive speech'. He features in a weird and wonderful tale in which he is carried off, with fourteen companions, on the back of a huge horse. Fionn sets off with fifteen men to track him down; they embark in 'a grand ship of great burthen' and, in the course of their journey, embroil themselves in conflict on an international scale, involving the king of India, the king of Africa, and, on the other side, the king of Greece. They discover that it was Ábartach, son of Alchad, who had caused Conán's abduction on the huge horse; in the Land of Promise they spot Ábartach in a grand gathering; when they threaten him with battle he agrees to restore to Fionn his missing men and to pay compensation. Conán, for his part, as his compensation, chooses fourteen women, 'best that there were in the Land of Promise', as well as Ábartach's own wife, all of them to be carried home on the great horse. There were half a dozen saints of the name, which is anglicised simply as *Conan*. Perhaps the name's most bizarre appearance is as 'Conán the Barbarian'.

CONCHOBAR, CONCHOBHAR *m*

A suggested meaning is 'wolf-lover' or 'lover of hounds'. Its most famous owner was Conchobhar mac Nessa, King of the Ulaid (Ulstermen), in the heroic period, with his royal seat at Emhain Macha (Navan, Co. Armagh). The exiled Ulster hero, Fergus mac Róich, said of him: 'This is how Conchobhar spends his time of sovereignty: one third of the day watching the youths, another third playing chess, another third drinking ale till he falls asleep from it. Though we have been exiled by him I

still maintain there is not in Ireland a warrior more wonderful.'
It was to the ageing Conchobhar that Deirdre was to be wed
before she arranged to elope with Naoise. Conchobhar's
jealousy led to the treacherous death of Naoise and the
suicide of Deirdre. The most acceptable English forms are
Connor or even *Conor*; it has no connection whatsoever with the
name *Cornelius*.

CONLÁED, CONLAODH *m*

It has been suggested that it is a compound of *connla* (prudent
or chaste) and *áedh* (fire) — both of which are singularly appropriate to one of its most distinguished bearers, St Conláed of
Kildare. The monastery of Kildare was initially founded by St
Brigit as an institution solely for nuns; it soon became a double
monastery, however, with nuns under an abbess and monks
under an abbot, sharing a common church but with separate
residential accommodation. With an increasing number of both
nuns and monks Brigit found it necessary to have a resident
bishop, and Conláed was appointed first bishop. He is recorded
as having been 'one of the three chief artisans' of Ireland and
chief craftsman to St Brigit. A perpetual fire was maintained at
Kildare, tended by nineteen nuns — one tradition is that it was
for the use of travellers and pilgrims, another that it was a
custom inherited from a pagan sanctuary on the site. Conláed is
supposed to have been killed by a wolf; in 800 a costly new
shrine of gold and silver was made for his relics; his Feast Day is
May 3rd. English forms in use are *Conleth* and *Conley*.

CONLETH *see* CONLÁED

CONLEY *see* CONLÁED

CONNELL *see* CONALL

CON(N)OR *see* CONCHOBAR

CORMAC *m*

Is regarded as being a compound of the early name *Corb*, which is thought to be connected with the word *corbaid* (defile) and *macc* (son). It was a name born by many of the legendary ancestors of Irish septs, such as Cormac mac Airt, ancestor of the Uí Néill. Two particularly famous Cormacs are closely associated with Cashel, Co. Tipperary: one is the Cormac Mac Carthaig who was king of Munster and builder of Cormac's Chapel; the other is Cormac mac Cuilennáin, a scholar in both Irish and Latin, who combined the offices of king and bishop. As a king he was, inevitably, involved in the politics of the day (which, equally inevitably, usually meant warfare with his neighbours). The culmination of his political and military career was in 908, when his forces were met at Belach-Mugna in southern Kildare; they were defeated by the Leinstermen and the Uí Néill and he himself lost his life. His decapitated body was buried at Castledermot, Co. Kildare. Of his ecclesiastical and academic career the most important relic is *Sanas Cormaic* (Cormac's Glossary), which consists of a collection of etymological glosses on Irish words as well a series of articles on antiquities, history and mythology. The English form is the same as the Irish, *Cormac*.

COWAL *see* COMHGHALL

DAIBHEAD, DÁIBHÍ *m*

A borrowing of the biblical *David* which, while not much used in Ireland must certainly have been well known among Irish clerics. Several Irish saints had connections with Wales, including St M'Áedhóg of Ferns who is, albeit improbably, said to have studied with St Dewi (David); and Welsh ecclesiastical terms, such as *llan*, appear in early Christian Irish place-names. More-over representations on Irish High Crosses of harpists are fre-quently considered to represent David and, in many instances, the instrument in question no way resembles the actual Irish harp. The death of Davidus, son of Farannán, son of Guaire, bishop of Armagh and legate of all Ireland, is recorded in the year 550 — unfortunately in Latin. The form usually used nowa-days is *Dáibhí*, the English is, of course, *David*.

DAIGH, DAIG *m*

Means 'flame' or 'fire'. Its best known bearer is St Daigh of Inishkeen, Co. Louth who was a nephew of St Molaisse of Devenish, Co. Fermanagh, under whose care he was placed as a child; his uncle took him one day to visit St Mochta at his monastery in Louth. On meeting Daigh St Mochta predicted: 'Many a church vessel and ornament in gold, in silver, in brass and iron, will proceed from that hand and many an elegant volume will it write.' And a famous craftsman Daigh did become; he worked for St Comhghall at Bangor and for St Ciarán at Clonmacnoise. It was said of him: 'One hundred and fifty bells, a triumphant achievement, with a stout hostful hundred of crosiers, with sixty whole gospels from the hand of Daigh alone'. He died in 587; his Feast Day is August 18th. There is no specifically English form.

DAIMÍNE, DAIMHÍN *m*

This name is derived from the word *dam* (deer or ox). It was particularly popular among the Airgialla (Oriel, the area occupied mainly by modern Co. Tyrone, but with extensions into Cos.

Derry, Fermanagh and Armagh). The death of Daimín Daimairgit, king of Airgialla, is recorded in 564, and that of his son Conall in 608. The best form in English would be *Davin*. It may also be the source of the name *Damien*.

DÁIRE *m*

Means 'fruitful' or 'fertile', and may have been the name of an early god of fertility or a bull-god of some sort. Certainly the bull-connection is present in the fact that the celebrated *Donn Cuailnge* (Brown Bull of Cooley) belonged to one Dáire mac Fiachna. When Medb and Ailill were comparing their possessions it emerged that Medb had no bull to compare with Ailill's *Findbennach*. Medb, on learning that there was 'a bull even better and more excellent than he in the province of Ulster' despatched Fergus mac Róth to Cuailnge to seek the loan of Donn Cuailnge, offering fifty heifers for a year's loan. At first Dáire was inclined to agree, but on getting the impression that if he did not grant the loan willingly, he would be compelled to grant it by the might of Medb's army, he changed his mind. His refusal to grant the loan was the proximate cause of the great fight between the Ulstermen and the men of Ireland, known as *Táin Bó Cuailnge*, in which Cú Chulainn played such an heroic role. *Darragh* or *Derry* might be used as anglicised forms.

DÁIRÍNE *f*

This name is probably derived from *dáire* (fruitful or fertile). One of its best known bearers was the younger of the two daughters of Túathal Teachtmar, legendary king of Tara. Eochaidh, king of Leinster, was married to the elder, Fithir. Eochaidh visited Túathal at Tara and reported that Fithir was dead; Túathal therefore allowed him to marry Dáiríne; when they arrived at Eochaidh's fortress, Dáiríne discovered to her horror that her elder sister was still alive, and both girls immediately died of shame. When the news reached Túathal he marched on Leinster and exacted a tribute. There is no specifically English form, though *Darina* might be used.

DAMHNAIT, DAMHNAT f

Means 'fawn'. The best known Damhnat is St Damhnat of Tedavnet (Damhnat's House), Co. Monaghan. She founded a monastery for women in Co. Monaghan in the sixth century. Her crosier, now preserved in the National Museum in Dublin, was formerly used for the testing of oaths. The punishment for swearing a false oath on the crosier was reckoned to be dire — the most usual result being that the mouth of the perjuror was turned permanently awry, making him, or her, instantly recognisable as a liar. This saint has been, on occasions, confused with Dympna of Gheel. Her Feast Day is June 13th; the best of the English versions is *Davnat* or *Devnat*.

DAMIEN *see* DAIMÍNE

DANA, DANU, ANA, ANU f

The name means 'wealth' or 'abundance' and she was the Irish goddess of abundance. The forms with initial 'D' are considered to be later scholarly modifications. She was described by Cormac mac Cuilennán, the tenth-century king bishop and scholar as 'the mother of the gods of Ireland'. Her name is preserved in the name of a pair of breast-shaped mountains in Co. Kerry, *Dá Chích Annan* (the breasts of Anu). Surprisingly enough in view of her pagan origins, her name is also that of a St Ana, whose Feast Day is on January 18th. The best English forms are *Ana* or, more recently, *Dana*.

DARINA *see* DÁIRINE

DARRAGH *see* DÁIRE

DAVID *see* DAIBHEAD

DAVIN *see* DAIMÍNE

DAVNAT *see* DAMHNAIT

DEAGLÁN, DECLÁN *m*

The most celebrated bearer of this name is Deaglán of Ardmore, Co. Waterford. He was one of the number of pre-Patrician missionaries in Ireland; having visited Rome and been consecrated by the Pope, he returned to Ireland, and, it is said, met Patrick on the way. Several of the miracles attributed to him concern a small black bell which he had received from Heaven, known as *Duibhín Deagláin*; it provided a ship for Deaglán and his followers when no other vessel could be found; on the last stage of the journey to Ireland it accompanied the ship on which the saint was travelling, overtook it as they approached land and, effectively, chose the spot at which Deaglán was to establish his monastery, on an island off the Waterford coast. Deaglán eventually caused the waters of the wide strait that separated his island from the mainland to recede, leaving many fine fish stranded. The divinely reclaimed land proved to be extremely fertile and helped support Deaglán and his community. The saint's grave is said to be in a small oratory at Ardmore which is a station of the annual pilgrimage held on his Feast Day, July 24th. The received anglicised form is *Declan*.

DEARBHÁIL, DERBÁIL/DEIRBHILE *f*

These originally separate names seem to have become conflated in modern usage. It has been suggested that the first is a compound meaning 'daughter of Fal' (*Fál* is a legendary name for Ireland), while the second is said to mean 'daughter of a poet'. Collectively they are represented by St Deirbhile of Fallmore, Co. Mayo, who founded a convent there in the sixth century. The name(s) became popular in the later medieval period when, for example, in 1343, we hear of Derbháil, daughter of Áedh O'Donnell going on a visit to Mac Dermot at Inishterry, Co. Roscommon; while there she was seized with a fatal sickness; on her death 'she was nobly and honourably interred in the monastery of Boyle. There never was born a woman of her tribe who surpassed her in goodness'. Another enjoyed a different fate: in 1339 the daughter of Turlough O'Brien, who was already wife of the son of the Earl of Ulster, was taken to wife by Turlough O'Conor, who put away Derbháil, daughter of Aodh O'Donnell. The anglicised forms are *Derval* or *Dervila*.

DEASÚN *see* DESMUMHNACH

DECLAN *see* DEAGLÁN

DEIRDRE *see* DERDRIU

DERDRIU, DEIRDRE f
Several meanings have been suggested for this name: some hold it to mean 'she who chatters', others that it may be a reduplicated form of an old word for 'woman'. The most famous owner of the name, of course, is Deirdre, the daughter of Feidlimid, who features in the most poignant of Irish tales, *The lamentable story of the sons of Uisliu*. Before her birth she cried from the womb, terrifying all that heard her. Cathbad the magician forecast that she would be the fairest of the women of Ireland but that, because of her, death and destruction would come upon the land of the Ulstermen. Conchobhar mac Nessa, the King of the Ulstermen, who was present, vowed that he would have her reared in isolation and would marry her himself when she was of age. And she was so reared, with only a poetess called Leborcham allowed to visit her and her foster-parents. One day she was watching her foster-father flaying a calf in the snow, while a raven drank the blood. She said, 'I could love a man with those three colours: hair as black as a raven's wing, cheeks the colour of blood and skin as white as the snow.' She asked Leborcham who such a man might be; Leborcham replied, 'That man is Naoise, the son of Usliu.' One day Deirdre was looking over the ramparts and spied a man who answered the prescription. They fell in love, and despite Conchobhar's intention that he was to marry her, Deirdre and Naoise eloped, accompanied by his two brothers. They fled to Scotland, where they

lived happily for several years. Conchobhar, growing increasingly bitter, pretended that he had forgiven them, and sent Fergus mac Róich as guarantor of their safety. By the exercise of guile Conchobhar separated them from Fergus; on arrival at Conchobar's court at Emhain Mhacha, Naoise was treacherously slain, along with his brothers, and Deirdre compelled to marry Conchobhar. The outcome was that Fergus went into voluntary exile with Medb in Connacht, and, after a year with Conchobhar during which she never smiled, Deirdre jumped out of a chariot and killed herself. From her grave and Naoise's, two pines grew and interlocked inseparably at the top. Her story was made popular by the poets and playwrights of the Celtic revival, including J.M. Synge, in his unfinished *Deirdre of the Sorrows*; the only acceptable form in English is *Deirdre* — there is no 'translation'.

DERINN *see* DOIRIND

DERMOT *see* DIARMAID

DERVAL *see* DEARBHÁIL

DERVILA *see* DEARBHÁIL

DESMOND *see* DESMUMHNACH

DESMUMHNACH *m*
It literally means 'man of Muman', a tribe or territory in the Cork area of Munster in the centuries preceding the Anglo-Norman invasion. Apparently there is but a single reference to an individual bearing the name, as a putative ancestor of the Cork family Ó *Deasmhumhnaigh*. The name was associated with the family of Mac Carthy, as kings of Desmond, and, of course later on with the FitzGeralds as Earls of Desmond. The English name *Desmond* seems to be the place-name lifted as a

personal name. To make the story even more bizarre the English *Desmond* seems to have been re-translated into Irish as *Deasún*.

DEVNAT *see* DAMHNAIT

DIARMAID, DIARMAIT *m*

No satisfactory meaning of this name has yet been offered. As well as being the name of the greatest lover in Irish literature, Diarmait úa Duibne, the hero of *The Pursuit of Diarmaid and Gráinne*, it was also the name of several Irish kings, including Diarmaid mac Cerbhal, who died in or about 565, and, of course, Diarmaid Mac Murrough, king of Leinster, who was responsible for inviting the Anglo-Normans to Ireland to assist him against his enemies. In 1152, when Tigernán Úa Ruairc had incited the enmity of both Turlough Ó Connor and Diarmaid Mac Murrough, in consequence of which Ua Ruairc was deprived of some of his recent conquests, Mac Murrough rubbed salt into Úa Ruairc's wound by abducting his wife, Dervorguilla; it is said that she was a more than willing victim and that Úa Ruairc was as difficult in love as he was in politics. In 1166 Mac Murrough, after being forced to submit to the new High King, Ruaidhrí Ó Connor, and suffering from the vengeful attack by Ó Ruairc on the small portion of his territories which remained to him, seeing no hope of recovery, sailed to England and put in motion the process by which the Anglo-Normans would establish themselves in Ireland. An accepted English form is *Dermot*.

DOIRIND, DÁIRINN *f*

It has been suggested that this name may mean 'daughter of Finn', i.e. *Der Finn*. Notwithstanding the meaning of the name it is as one of three daughters of Midhir Yellow-mane, the others being Aoife and Aillbhe, that we meet Doirind. The three were given as wives to Ruidhe, Fiacha and Eochaid, sons of Lughaid Menn, the king of Ireland 'since from wives it is that either fortune or misfortune is derived', in addition to rather generous presents (thrice fifty ounces of red gold from each of one hundred and fifty sons of kings as a starter). English forms could be either *Derinn*, *Dorren* or *Doreen*. *Dorothy* has been used as a totally erroneous English equivalent.

DOMNALL, DOMHNALL, DÓNAL *m*

Meaning 'world-mighty', it was a very popular name in ancient Ireland. Among its bearers were no less than five High Kings. In 1039 one Domnall, Domnall son of Donnchad, King of Úi-Fáeláin, was slain by another Domnall, Domnall Úa Fergaile, King of Fortuatha-Laigen (the borders of Leinster). A mere four years later this second Domnall was slain by his own people. In 764 another Domnall, Domnall Mide, a High King of the Southern Úi Néill, was the cause of a bizarre situation; on his death in 763 he had been buried at Durrow 'with honour and veneration', while his ancestors had been buried at Clonmacnoise. The monks of Clonmacnoise, endowed with a high degree of world-liness, were aghast at the prospect of losing much revenue from such a drastic change in burial custom; they marched against their commercial rivals of Durrow, slaughtering two hundred of them. There were at least three saints of the name. The best English form is *Donal*.

DONAGH *see* DONNCHAD

DONNCHAD, DONNCHADH, DONNCHA *m*

A compound of the word *donn* (brown) and meaning 'brown lord'. One particularly notable example of the name is as that of the son of Brian Boru, king of Munster from 1014 (when his father was slain at Clontarf) until 1064, when he died in Rome; an inscription on the *cumdach* (case or shrine) of the Stowe Missal requests a prayer for him, while another inscription on the left-hand edge of the base records that the missal was made by Dunchad úa Taccáin of the community of Clon-macnoise. This by no means completes the association of bearers of the name Donnchad with important pieces of ecclesiastical metalwork, for we know that the metal shrine of the *Book of Armagh* was commissioned by the High King, Donnchad, son of Flann Sinna, in 939. The name has been acceptably anglicised as *Donagh* or *Donough*.

DONNFHLAIDH, DUNFLAITH *f*

A name meaning 'brown princess'. It is recorded rarely but a Dunlaith, daughter of Fogartach, died in 773; and a Dunflaith, daughter of Flaithbertach, a king of Ireland who died as a cleric in 764, died in 798. The name has achieved great popularity in recent years. The best English form is *Dunla*.

DOREEN *see* DOIRIND

DOROTHY *see* DOIREND

DORRENN *see* DOIRIND

DOUGAL *see* DUBGALL

DOUGLAS *see* DUBHGHLAS

DUALD *see* DUBALTACH

DUBALTACH, DUBHALTACH, DUALTACH *m*

The meaning is generally accepted to be 'black-jointed' or 'dark-limbed'. It is, perhaps, appropriate, that its most famous owner, Dubultach Mac Fir Bisigh, was, himself, a genealogist as well as an historian. He was born in the last decade of the sixteenth century at Lackan Castle, Co. Sligo, of a family of hereditary historians. He studied law and history in schools in Co. Tipperary and Clare, and during this time made a copy of the Annals of Ossory and Leinster. He lost his father in 1643 and the family estate in the course of the wars of 1641/43; he then moved to Galway, where he commenced work on the genealogy of Irish families. He then went to Dublin, where he was employed as a translator and copyist of important Irish manuscripts, including *Chronicon Scotorum* — a manuscript composed/compiled in the scriptoria of Clonmacnoise, Co. Offaly. In this notable work he was supported by the historian Sir James Ware. He was slain in an affray in an inn in Co. Sligo in 1670. He has rightly been described as 'the last real scholar of the old order'. His name can best be anglicised as *Dualta* or *Duald*; *Dudley* is not really appropriate.

DUBGALL, DUBGHALL *m*

This name means 'dark, or black, foreigner'; it was applied by the Irish to the Vikings, particularly the Danes, whose coming to Dublin in 850 is referred to in the Annals. It was popular even among the Irish, particularly in the North. Dubhgall son of Donnchad, royal heir of Ailech, was killed by his kinsman, Muiredach son of Flann, in 879. Among the Vikings slain at the Battle of Clontarf, in 1014, however, was Dubhgall, son of Amlaimh. The best English form is *Dougal*.

DUBHGHLAS *m*

This name is a compound of *dubh* (black and *glas* (blue). Despite the fact that it was actually more popular in Scotland than in Ireland, one very distinguished Irish bearer of it was the first President of Ireland, Douglas Hyde. He was born at Castlerea, Co. Roscommon, in 1860. He was educated at Trinity College, Dublin, where he won prizes for English prose and verse. In 1891 he went to Canada for a year as a Professor of Modern Languages; returning to Ireland he settled in Co. Roscommon, and devoted himself particularly to the revival of the Irish language, which he himself had learned from the people. He collected folklore and songs from them, which provided the material for his first two books *Beside the Fire* (1889) and *Love Songs of Connacht* (1893). He helped to found the Gaelic League in

1893 and became its first president. It played a vital role in the revival of a sense of national identity. In 1909 he was appointed the first Professor of Modern Irish in University College, Dublin. When the Constitution of 1937 created the post of President of Ireland he was unanimously elected and held the office until 1945, when his term expired. He died in Dublin in 1949. *Douglas* is, of course, the received English form.

DUDLEY *see* DUBALTACH

DUNLA *see* DONNFHLAIDH

E

ÉAMONN, ÉAMANN *m*

An Irish version of the English name E*dmond*, introduced to Ireland by the Anglo-Normans, where it became quite popular. It would be difficult not to cite Éamon de Valera as one of the most distinguished bearers of the name, despite the fact that he was born, in 1882, in New York of a Spanish father and an Irish mother. On the death of his father in 1884 he was sent to Ireland to be reared by his grandmother near Ráth Lúirc in Co. Cork, where he was introduced to patriotism by his parish priest. He graduated in mathematics and taught the subject at several colleges. In 1908 he joined the Gaelic League; one of his teachers was Sinéad Flanagan, whom he married in 1910. In 1913 he joined the Volunteers and as adjutant of the Dublin Brigade in 1916, participated in the Easter Rising, occupying Boland's Mill. After the surrender he was court-martialled, convicted and sentenced to death; he was reprieved and released in 1917. He then easily won a by-election in Co. Clare and went on to be elected President by the first Dáil Éireann in 1919. The Anglo-Irish Treaty of 1921 was not acceptable to de Valera and in the bitter Civil War that followed he and his followers were defeated. In 1926 he founded the Fianna Fáil party and devoted himself to making the concept of an independent Irish Republic a reality. In 1959 he was elected President of Ireland, an office which he held for the maximum period allowed, fourteen years. He died two years later in 1975. The proper English version is, of course, E*dmond*, but E*dward* is almost universally regarded as a suitable equivalent.

ÉANNA, ÉNNAE

There is a medieval suggestion that the name means 'birdlike'. It was borne by a number of legendary heroes, including Énnae Airgthech, a legendary king of Munster of whom it is said that he had made shields of silver which he distributed to his chiefs. The most famous Énnae, however, was Énnae of Aran. He was born in Co. Meath, where his father, Ainmire, was a chieftain;

46

he succeeded his father until his sister, St Fainche, persuaded him to become a cleric. He trained at Candida Casa, in Galloway, before returning to Ireland to found his church on Inishmore, the largest of the Aran Islands. His Feast Day is March 21st. The accepted anglicisation is E*nda*.

ÉBLIU, ÉIBHLIU, ÉBLENN, ÉIBHLEANN f

It is supposed to be derived from an Old Irish word *óiph* meaning 'beauty, sheen or radiance'; it is also believed by some to be another name for the sun goddess. One legendary Éibhliu, daughter of Guaire, was married to Mairid, son of Caraid, described as a 'good' king of Munster. She took a fancy to one of Mairid's sons, Eochaid, and after importuning him steadily for some time persuaded him to elope with her. When they reached the *brugh* of the *mac óg* (the cluster of Passage Tombs in the Boyne Valley) a tall man came out to them and killed all their horses; at their pleading he supplied them with one very large horse, on which they loaded all their gear. He warned them not to stop or unload the horse until they reached their destination in Ulster. Here they stopped at a spring well which, because of carelessness, overflowed, creating Lough Neagh, drowning Eochaid and all his family save three. Éibhliu is said to have given her name to Slieve Eibhlinne in Co. Tipperary. The recommended English forms are E*vle* or E*vlin*.

ECHNA f

It is considered to be derived from *ech* (steed). One Echna was a daughter of Muiredach mac Fínnachta, king of Leinster. 'The manner of this lady was this: she had three perfections; for of the whole world's wise women she was one, and he whom she should have counselled had as the result both affluence and consideration.' She seems to have had a *penchant* for the good life. When we, and Caeilte (one of the chief warriors of the Fianna who miraculously returns from the Otherworld to recount to St Patrick some of the chief exploits of the Fianna), meet her, she is in the company of nine lovely women: 'A smock of royal silk she had next to her skin; over that an outer tunic of soft silk and around her a hooded mantle of crimson fastened on her breast with a golden brooch.' They were playing chess and had a vessel of delicious mead at hand. Every time they finished a game they had a draught of mead; 'they caroused, in fact, and made merry'. There is no recognised English form.

EDMOND *see* ÉAMONN

EDWARD *see* ÉAMONN

EGAN *see* ÁEDUCÁN

EIBHLÍN, AIBHÍLÍN f
Irish forms of the names *Avelina, Evelina* and *Emeline* introduced by the Franks, or Anglo-Normans. It is probably best known in the seventeenth-century song *Eibhlín a rún*, written by the poet and harper Cearbhall Ó Dálaigh to express his love for Eibhlín Kavanagh (and with which he persuaded her to elope with him on her very wedding day!). Funnily enough the best-known bearer of it has also a musical association; she was Eibhlín Dubh ní Chonaill who, being widowed after a childhood marriage to an elderly husband, fell desperately in love with the dashing Art Ó Laoghaire, just returned from serving as a captain in the Hungarian Hussars. They married against her family's wishes and had two sons. The trouble came when the High Sheriff of Cork, Abraham Morris, offered twenty pounds reward for the apprehension of Ó Laoghaire. It seems likely that Ó Laoghaire stood trial and was acquitted, but when his horse won all before it at Macroom races in 1773, actually beating a horse belonging to Morris, the High Sheriff seized his opportunity. He offered Ó Laoghaire five pounds for the winning horse (this was, by law, the maximum value permitted for a horse owned by a Catholic); Ó Laoghaire, naturally, refused and was immediately

proscribed. Ó Laoghaire was killed by a soldier under Morris's command, and Eibhlín, on the very spot where he was murdered, began to compose for him the most beautiful of all Irish laments, *Caoineadh Airt Úi Laoghaire*. The most acceptable English forms are *Eileen*, *Aileen*, *Evelyn*, *Evelina* or even *Emeline*.

EILIS f

A derivative of the medieval French *Isabel* (Elizabeth), introduced into Ireland by the Franks. It was quite a common name in medieval Ireland. One Eilis, Eilis nic Diarmada Rua, was made famous by the blind harper Toirdhealbach Ó Cearbhalláin (Turlough Ó Carolan), probably the granddaughter of Ó Carolan's oldest and dearest patrons, the McDermott Roes of Ballyfarnon, Co. Roscommon, whom Ó Carolan describes as 'outshining the rose in beauty'. It can be translated back into *Elizabeth*, or retain the form *Eilis* even in English contexts.

EIMER, ÉMER f

She was a daughter of Forgall Manach and was said to possess 'the six gifts of womanhood — the gift of beauty; the gift of voice; the gift of sweet speech; the gift of needlework; the gift of wisdom and the gift of chastity'. Cú Chulainn caught sight of her at her father's fortress and immediately fell in love with her and sought her in marriage; Émer replied that although she returned his love she would not marry before her elder sister Fial; her father Forgall was, in any event, against the match on the grounds that Cú Chulainn still had his reputation to win. Cú Chulainn went off to Scotland to train in the art of war. During his absence Forgall tried to marry Émer off to a southern king called Lugaid mac Ros; but Lughaid, who had heard of Cú Chulainn's reputation as a warrior, declined the offer. When Cú Chulainn returned he presented himself at Forgall's fortress and was refused admittance; he leapt over the defences and slaughtered twenty-four of Forgall's warriors; Forgall himself leapt to his death from the rampart. Cú Chulainn carried Émer off with two loads of gold and silver. There is no separate English form, but E*mer* seems the most popular in modern usage.

ÉIMHÍN, ÉMÍNE *m & f*

This name is possibly connected with the word *éim* (prompt, ready). The best known bearer of the name is St Éimhín, one of the six sons of Eoghan mac Murchad of the royal house of Munster, all six of whom took up the religious life and went on to found monasteries. The place where Éimhín founded his is now known as Monasterevan, Co. Kildare. He died there in 689 and is buried there. His Feast Day is December 22nd. The name has increasingly become a name for girls as well as boys. It could be anglicised as E*vin* or E*van*.

EIRNÍN, ERNÍNE *m & f*

It has been suggested that it may be derived from *iarn* (iron). There are some sixteen saints of this name, but little is known of any of them, except that one was a virgin daughter of one Archenn with a Feast Day on February 28th, while St Eirnín Cass (curly-haired) was associated with Leighlin, Co. Carlow. E*rnin* is probably the best anglicisation.

EITHNE *f*

Possibly connected with the word *eithne* (kernel, of a nut) but also possibly from *aitten*, meaning gorse and the third most popular name given to women in early Ireland. Eithne was the mother of the god Lugh — the god of the sun and of all arts and crafts. The name recurs as the name of the wives of various kings both legendary (Conn Cétchathach) and historical (Congalach mac Máelmithidh, high-king, who was killed by Vikings in 955); as that of mothers of saints (both Colmcille and Áedán, or Máedhóg) and as that of saints. Eithne and Fidelma, two daughters of King Laoghaire, were summarily instructed, baptised, ordained and 'sanctified' in one day by St Patrick when they encountered him in 433, sharing the shortest, strangest and most poignant life of any saints in the history of the Irish

Church. As the end of the story says, 'they quitted their earthly tabernacle and went to meet their heavenly Spouse, sweetly falling asleep in the Lord'. Their Feast Day is January 11th; although the name has been anglicised as *Annie*, a name with which it has no connection, there seems little need to anglicise it at all.

ELIZABETH *see* EILIS

EMELINE *see* EIBHLÍN

ENAT *see* ÁEDNAT

ENDA *see* ÉANNA

ENYA *see* ÁINE

EÓGAN, EOGHAN *m*
Means 'born of the yew'; it was a very popular name among the early Irish. Among the tribal ancestors bearing the name was Eoghan, son of Niall of the Nine Hostages, who gave his name to the *Cénel Eoghain*, as a result of which it is now enshrined in the name of Co. Tyrone (Tír Eoghain). It was also popular among early saints such as Eoghan of Ardstraw, Co. Tyrone, who while studying at Clones was captured by pirates and carried off to Britain; he escaped and continued his studies at the celebrated Candida Casa, in Galloway. He returned to Ireland, founded the monastery of Kilnamanagh, near Tallaght, before establishing his monastery at Ardstraw. Understandably he had an interest in releasing captives. His Feast Day is August 23rd; acceptable English forms are *Owen* and *Eugene* (though the latter is, in fact, an independent name of Greek derivation).

EOIN *m*
An early borrowing of the biblical name *Johannes*. An eminent bearer of the name was Eoin MacNeill, patriot and scholar.

Born at Glenarm, Co. Antrim in 1867 he became deeply interested in the study of early Irish history. He helped found the
Gaelic League in 1893. In 1908 he was appointed a professor
of early Irish history at U.C.D. Through his involvement with
the Gaelic League he was elected chairman of the council that
formed the Irish Volunteers in 1913, later becoming Chief of
Staff. He was against military action, and, indeed, tried to
countermand the mobilisation of Volunteers for the Easter
Rising in 1916. Nonetheless, after the surrender he, with many
others, was arrested and sentenced to penal servitude for life.
He supported the Anglo-Irish Treaty of 1921 and became Minister
of Education in the first government of the Irish Free State. He
became disenchanted with politics and devoted himself to
scholarship, becoming chairman of the Irish Manuscripts Com-
mission in 1927. His major publications were *Phases of Irish History*
(1919) and *Celtic Ireland* (1921). The English form of *Eoin* is *John*.

ERNIN *see* EIRNÍN

ÉTAÍN, ÉADAOIN f
Thought to be connected with the word *ét* (jealousy) and thought
by some authorities to have been a sun-goddess. While there
are several Étaíns, including at least one saint, the best known
must be the heroine of *Tochmar Étaíne* (The Wooing of Étaín).
Étaín Echraidhe was daughter of Ailill, a king among the Ulaidh
(Ulstermen) and was judged to be the fairest and gentlest and
most beautiful woman in Ireland. Now a man called Mider,
knowing that Étaín was the fairest woman in Ireland, despite
the fact that he already had a wife called Fuamnach, had
extracted a promise from Áengus (Mac Occ) that she would be
obtained for him — which eventually she was, in return for the
clearing of twelve plains, the diversion of twelve rivers and her
weight in gold and silver. Needless to say Fuamnach was not
pleased when Mider arrived home with the fairest woman in
Ireland. Being, as they said, 'a woman of dreadful sorcery', she

turned poor Étaín first into a pool of water, this turned into a worm, which then turned into a scarlet fly — albeit a fly of great beauty and boundless enchantment, which accompanied Mider everywhere. For twice seven years Fuamnach caused the poor fly, which was Étaín, to be blown around Ireland until, at last, it fell into a goblet and was consumed, with the goblet's contents, by the wife of Étar. The fly was subsequently reborn, and, in time, became the woman of Echu Airem, king of Eriu. After many more miraculous adventures and devious machinations she was restored again to Mider. Her name can be anglicised as A*idin*, but E*tain* is used as well.

EUGENE *see* EÓGAN

EUNAN *see* ADOMNÁN

EVELYN *see* EIBHLÍN

EVIN *see* ÉIMHÍN

EVLE *see* ÉBLIU

EVLIN *see* ÉBLIU

FAINCHE *f*

The best known owner of this name was St Fainche of Rossory, Co. Fermanagh. She was sister to St Éanna of Aran. She had an ardent suitor, in the form of Óengus mac Natfraích, an early king of Cashel. Being certain that her own destiny lay in the religious life, she subtly — and successfully — diverted his affection and attention towards her sister Dáiríne. Having thus divested herself of her suitor she proceeded to establish her monastery at Rossory, on the shore of Lough Erne, in Co. Fermanagh. On the death of his father, Éanna was intending to take on his father's role, and, accompanied by some of his supporters, came to visit Fainche at Rossory. She, however, had other notions about Éanna's future, and persuaded him that he, too, should adopt the religious life. On her advice he left Ireland to pursue his studies in Galloway, Scotland; she learned of his piety and devotion from some visitors at Rossory and went to visit him, advising him as she left that if he was intent on returning to Ireland he should go to Aran; this he subsequently did. She did not survive long after her return. Her Feast Day is January 1st; her name does not really 'translate', so that *Fainche* is not only the Irish but the English form; *Fanny* seems irreverent as well as irrelevant.

FANNY *see* FAINCHE

FAOLÁN, FÁELÁN *m*

This name means 'wolf'. One distinguished bearer of it was an Ulsterman (his mother, a daughter of the king of Leinster, was to become St Kentigerna) who was baptised by St Ibhor and joined his monastery; he built a cell near the monastery and one night when supper was ready a servant was despatched to call him for his meal. The servant approached the darkened cell and, peering through a chink observed that the only light-source was Faolan's left hand, which emitted enough light for his right hand to write. He went off to Scotland as a missionary; a number of churches in Scotland are dedicated to him. His Feast Day is January 9th; in Scotland he is known as *Fillan* — which is probably the most satisfactory English form of the name.

FECHÍNE, FECHÍN *m*

Two different derivations have been offered for this name: one derives it from *fiach* (raven), the other from an old root meaning 'battle'. Of the five saints with the name the best known is St Fechín of Fore, Co. Westmeath. He received his education at Achonry, Co. Sligo, where he caused water to flow from dry soil, creating a well that was known ever after as 'the well of St Fechín'. He left Achonry and founded monasteries at Fore, at Cong, Co. Mayo, at Termonfeckin, Co. Louth and others in Co. Galway and Co. Sligo. In one monastery two of his monks died of starvation and the rest were threatened with the same fate until relief was sent by King Guaire of Connacht. This he was able to repay years later when the king's son, Rónán, who suffered from a chronic headache for which he had sought a cure from physicians not only in Ireland but in Britain as well, came to visit him. Through the prayers and blessings of Fechín, the lad was quickly restored to full health. At Fore, Fechín had a rule which excluded women — even milkmaids — totally from the monastic area. He died of the yellow plague in 664 or 665. His Feast Day is January 20th; *Fechin* is considered the best English form.

FEDELM, FEIDHELM *f*

A name borne by many famous women in ancient Ireland. One of the most interesting was Fedelm Noíchrothach (the nine-times beautiful) who was a female warrior notable for her great beauty. She was a daughter of Conchobhar mac Nessa, king of Ulster. She was married to Cairpre Nia Fer, by whom she had a son, Erc. She eloped with Conall Cearnach, foster-brother and blood cousin of Cú Chulainn, whose death he avenged. The form in English is normally the Latin form, *Fidelma*.

FEDELMID, FEIDHLIMIDH, FEIDHELM *m & f*

One proffered explanation for this name is that it means 'ever good'. One Feidhlim Rechtmar was the grandfather of the mother of St Molaisse of Devenish. There were several saints of the name, including Feidhlimidh of Kilmore, Co. Cavan, whose own mother, a grand-daughter of Dubtach úa Lugáir, chief poet to King Laoghaire, is said to have been married four times, with no fewer than six sons and one daughter taking up the religious life and becoming saints. His Feast Day is August 9th. It was, too, a popular name among historical kings and princes; at least three early kings of Munster bore it. One northern prince with the name was Sir Phelim O'Neill who, in 1641, led an uprising in Ulster 'in which the long-oppressed fury of the native race found vent in cruel massacres of the planters'. He was executed as a traitor in 1653. The English version of the name for males is *Phelim* or *Felim*, for females *Fidelma* is probably the best substitute for an English form.

FELIM *see* FEDELMID

FENELLA *see* FIONNUALA

FENIT *see* FÉTHNAID

FENNORE *see* FINNABHAIR

FERGAL, FEARGHAL *m*

Connected with *fear* (man) and meaning 'manly' or 'valorous', it was an extremely popular name among the early Irish. Clearly living up to his name, according to the Annals, was Fergal mac Máeldúin, who became king of Ireland in 709. Even before this he and two companions had 'murdered' Indrechtach, son of Murchad, king of Connacht. In 717 he slew Conall Grant, the victor of the battle of Kells, and in 720 is recorded as being responsible for the wasting of Leinster and the exaction of tribute and hostages before himself being slain at the Hill of Allen by

Murchad mac Brain. This, of course, was quite normal activity for an Irish king of the period. The anglicised form would be simply *Fergal*.

FERGUS, FEARGHUS *m*

A name meaning 'the strength of a man'; it was a very common name in ancient Ireland and was borne by at least ten saints. Perhaps the most exemplary bearer of the name was Fergus mac Róich, one-time king of Ulster, dupe, man of principle and one of the prominent personages in *Táin Bó Cuailgne*. Having been duped out of the kingship of Ulster in favour of Conchobhar, Fergus was content enough to serve under him until he was sent by Conchobhar to persuade Deirdre, whom Conchobhar had hoped to marry, and Naoise, with whom she had eloped, to return to Ireland under the surety of Fergus. When Conchobhar had Naoise murdered in the absence of Fergus, Fergus went into exile with a band of dissidents, taking refuge with Medb and Ailill in Connacht and so, in the conflict between the Ulstermen and the men of Ireland, was on the opposite side to his former friends and comrades. His pact with Cú Chulainn that they should never engage in single combat eventually led to the defeat of the army of Medb and Ailill. The form in English is simply *Fergus*.

FÉTHNAID, FÉTHNAT *f*

No interpretation seems to have been offered of this name. She was daughter of Fidach and a musician of the Tuatha dé Danaan. We are given a picture of her at work: a gentle and yellow-haired damsel, sitting in a chair in the middle of the mansion, holding a harp on which she performed and played continually; every time she played a lay a horn was offered to her from which she took a draught. Her death was one of the three losses of the Tuatha. The name could be anglicised as *Fenit*.

FIACHRA *m*

The meaning is thought to be 'battle-king'. One of the most poignantly portrayed bearers of the name in legend is Fiachra, son of Lir, the sea-god, by his first wife, Aobh; he and his two brothers and one sister (i.e. 'The Children of Lir') were turned into swans by Lir's second wife, Aoife, Aobh's sister. The name was also borne by a number of saints, among who was St Fiachra of Ullard, Co. Kilkenny, who is said to have administered the last rites to St Comhghall of Bangor and brought his arm back to Kilkenny to be enshrined as a relic. He went to France where he died in 670 at Meaux. He gave his name to a Parisian horse-cab. His Feast Day is February 8th; the English — and French — form of his name is *Fiacre*.

FIDELMA *see* FEDELM *or* FEDELMID

FILLAN *see* FAOLÁN

FINIAN *see* FINNÉN

FINN, FIONN *m & f*
Means 'fair, brilliant white' and is the name of a number of legendary heroes. The best known of these is Finn mac Cumall, who started his career as Demna, the orphaned son of Cumal. He was sent to be educated by a sage called Finegas, whose ambition in life was to catch the Salmon of Knowledge, which lived in a pool in the River Boyne; eventually he succeeded and gave the fish to his pupil to cook; as Demna was doing so, he burned his hand on the hot flesh and, because he sucked his hand to cool it, it was he who obtained the knowledge or wisdom the salmon contained. In consequence he was dubbed Finn. As a reward for saving the royal palace at Tara from a demon, he was made leader of the Fianna — a sort of royal bodyguard — by Cormac mac Airt, the High King. He had two hounds, Bran and Sceolan, who were in fact, his own nephews, being the offspring of his bewitched sister. As leader of the Fianna he had many adventures, inevitably involving much fighting and hunting, with a heavy mixture of magic and sorcery.

In his old age he was given Gráinne, daughter of Cormac, as his wife; she however did not much care for marriage to an elderly gentleman, and promptly eloped with Diarmaid. Needless to say Finn, in his turn, did not much care for this, and so ensued the 'Pursuit of Diarmaid and Gráinne'. Of the two forms above, *Finn* would be the obvious anglicised one.

FINNABHAIR, FIONNABAIR, FIONÚIR f

'White ghost' or 'white sprite' has been offered as a possible meaning. One legendary bearer of the name was daughter of Conchobhar mac Nessa: she was one of the three wives of Celtchair mac Uithechar, an Ulster warrior and comrade of Conchobhar in *Táin Bó Cuailgne*. Another Fionnabhair was a daughter of Medb and Ailill. A suggested English form is *Fennore*.

FINNBARR, FIONNBHARR m

Meaning 'fair-haired' it was the name of a number of saints, the best known of whom is undoubtedly St Finnbarr of Cork. He was born in Co. Cork, the son of a metal-worker, at a place which has been identified with the fort of Lisnacaheragh, near Garranes, which, indeed, excavation showed to have been the site of metal-working on a large scale. He had early encounters with a king called Fachtna, for whom he performed two miraculous cures: first he cured the king's blind son and mute daughter; then he restored the king's wife to life. He also caused nuts to grow on a tree in spring-time, as a display of divine power. He founded a monastery at Gougane Barra, near the source of the River Lee before travelling downstream to found another, on a site indicated to him by the Angel of God, on the south bank of the river, on a hill-slope south-west of the present city of Cork. His consecration was accompanied by an unusual type of miracle: he and his teacher, Meccuirp, were raised by angels and let down by the altar; from the ground nearby oil broke forth, covering the feet of those standing there. He died at Cloyne, probably in 623, and his body was translated to Cork to be deposited in a silver shrine. His Feast Day is September 25th; Irish 'pet' forms, *Barre* and *Bairre*, are commonly used, particularly of the Cork saint. The normal English forms are *Finbar* or *Finnbar*, while the 'pet' form, *Bairre*, is rendered as *Barry* in English.

FINNÉN, FINNIAN *m*

Is derived from Irish *finn* (fair, pale-coloured). Several Irish saints bore the name, of which the best known are Finian of Movilla and Finnian of Clonard. The first studied, as did so many early Irish churchmen, at Candida Casa, at Whithorn in Galloway, Scotland, and, after a visit to Rome, founded a monastery at the head of Strangford Lough, Co. Down. His reputation for scholarship attracted many pupils, including Colmcille; it was his manuscript that Colmcille copied, leading to the famous copyright judgment by the High King 'To every cow its calf, to every book its copy'; his Feast Day is September 10th. The other most famous Finnian was Finnian of Clonard, Co. Meath, who, while specialising in most severe austerity and mortification, was also renowned for his scholarship; the oldest Irish penitential, the *Penitential of Vinnianus*, is considered to have been written by him; his Feast Day is December 12th. The most usual English forms are *Finnian* or *Finian*.

FINNSECH, FINNSEACH *f*

Means 'fair lady' or 'blonde lady'. There are two saints of this name of whom little other than their names and dates are known. St Finnsech of Trim, Co. Meath, has her Feast Day on February 17th and St Finnsech of Urney, Co. Tyrone, has hers on October 13th. A possible English form would be *Finsha*.

FINOLA *see* FIONNUALA

FINSHA *see* FINNSECH

FINTAN, FIONTAN *m*

Two meanings have been suggested for this name: 'the white ancient' and 'white fire'; there are over seventy Irish saints bearing it. Of these one of the best known is Fintan moccu Échdach of Clonenagh, Co. Laois, a monastery which he founded after studying with St Colmán at Terryglass, Co. Tipperary. He had a reputation for recruiting disciples in rather unorthodox fashion: he once persuaded a man called Fergna, who had a virtuous and beloved wife, twelve sons and seven daughters 'to abandon this world's pleasures and assume the religious habit'. He died in 603; his Feast Day is February 17th. Another well known saintly Fintan was Fintan moccu Moie, of Taghmon, Co. Wexford, who as a child came under the influence of a hermit who taught him to read and write; while he studied with the hermit two wolves guarded his father's sheep for him. He studied with St Comhghall at Bangor, visited Iona, and then came back to Ireland to found a monastery at Taughmon (Munnu's house, Mo-Fhinnu or Munnu being his 'pet-name') and another, with the same name, at Taghmon, Co. Wexford. At a synod held about 630 to discuss the date of Easter, Fintan was the principal spokesman for the traditionalists against the modernists led by Laisrén of Leighlin. This Fintan died in 635; his Feast Day is October 21st. The English form is simply *Fintan*.

FIONA *see* LASAIRFHÍONA

FIONNUALA, FIONNGUALA *f*

Means 'fair-shouldered' and was a very popular name in Ireland especially in the later medieval period. One Fionnghuala who went to considerable expense to be remembered was Fionnghuala, the daughter of O'Brien, who, with her husband the O'Donnell (Aodh Ruad, son of Niall Garve O'Donnell), endowed in 1474 the monastery of Donegal, granted by them 'to God and the friars of St Francis for the prosperity of their own souls and that the monastery might be a burial-place for them and their descendants'. Another memorable Fionnghuala features in an incident in 1418 when Richard, the son of Tomas O'Reilly, Lord of East Breifne, was drowned in Lough Sheelin. With him were also drowned his own son, Eoghan O'Reilly; Philip, son of Gilla-Isa, son of Godfrey O'Reilly, Dean of Drumlane and Vicar of Annagh, and many other distinguished persons. Fionnghuala, however, the wife of Richard O'Reilly and daughter of Mac Raghnall, escaped by swimming. The best anglicised forms are Finnuala or Finola (though Finvola is commonly used in Co. Derry and Fenella in Scotland); Nuala, a diminutive form, has become very popular — but it does appear quite early: Nuala, sister of Ruaidhrí O'Donnell, accompanied him on the ship which left Lough Swilly in 1507, carrying them into exile.

FLANN *m & f*

This is another of the names cited in the 'Rule' of St Máel Rúain as being suitable for a child of either sex. It means 'bright red' or 'blood red'. Flann, son of Áedh, son of Dlutach, was one of the combatants killed in a battle near Kells, Co. Meath, in 713. Another Flann, this time a cleric, an abbot of Armagh, died in the following year. One of the most illustrious Flanns, however, was Flann son of Máelsechlain, son of Máel-runaidh, son of Donnchad, also known as Flann Sinna, king of Tara, who died in the 68th year of his age, in 916, after reigning 'for 36 years, 6 months and five days'. He has the added distinction of being commemorated on one of the High Crosses at Clonmacnoise, Co. Offaly, known as 'The Cross of King Flann' because of a partially defaced inscription. It is also known as 'The Cross of the Scriptures'. A female called Flann, daughter of Donnchad, queen of Ailech, died in 939. A diminutive, Flannacán, was also in use. Despite the fact that it was anglicised, ineptly, as Florence, there is no real English form for it.

FODLA, FODHLA *f*

One of three ladies of the Tuatha dé Danaan (the people of the goddess Dana), the others being Banba and Éire, described as 'one of their shapely women', was married to Mac Cecht, son of Ogma, the god of eloquence. Like her sister, Éire, her name was used of Ireland. She also gave her name to Atholl, *Ath-Fhotla*, in Scotland. The form in English would be *Fola*.

FRANCIS/ES *see* PROINNSEAS

GARBÁN, GARBHÁN *m*

This name is derived from *garb* (rough). There were several early saints of this name, about none of whom very much is known. One was St Garbhán either of Kinsale, Co. Cork, or of Kinsealy, Co. Dublin, whose Feast Day is July 9th. A Garbhán of Meath died in 701. The best English form would be *Garvan*.

GARVAN *see* GARBÁN

GEARALT, GARALT, GEARÓID *m*

All, apparently, versions of a Teutonic name meaning 'spear-might', introduced to Ireland by the Anglo-Normans, among whom it was popular. It had, however, appeared in Ireland as early as the seventh or eighth century. The death of Garaalt, pontiff of Mayo of the Saxons, an Englishman, is recorded in 731. Needless to say it was a name later particularly favoured among the Fitz Geralds. One of the Fitz Geralds, Gearóid Iarla (the Earl), in the fourteenth century, was reputed to be the product of the rape, by his father, Muirís, of Áine the Love Goddess. Notwithstanding this he is described as 'a nobleman of wonderful bounty, cheerfulness in conversation, easy of access, charitable in deeds, a witty and ingenious composer of Irish music . . . '. He did write courtly love-poetry. After his death various traditions grew up about him — for example that he was not really dead, but merely sleeping and that in time of Ireland's peril he would rise again from the waters of Lough Gur. The English form is *Gerald*.

GEARARD *m*

A name confusingly similar to the above, and with a similar meaning, 'spear-brave'. The two may, indeed, have been on occasions confused; it seems nowadays to be the preferred version in Ireland. The English form is, of course, *Gerard*.

GEOFFREY *see* SÉAFRAID

GERALD *see* GEARALT

GERARD *see* GEARARD

GOBBÁN, GOBÁN *m*

This name is considered to be either a pet-form of *goba* (smith) or else a derivative of *Goibniu* (from the same root), an ancient Irish god of craftsmanship, who in later legend appears as Gobbán Saor, the master-craftsman of Irish folklore — who was credited, for example, with building the Round Towers. In the name of Goibniu he was capable of making a sword or a spear with three blows of his hammer. On one occasion an enemy spy came to see how he achieved this, seized one of the weapons he had made and drove it straight through Goibniu. Goibniu paused to kill the spy and then made his way to the god of medicine who cured his wound. There are several saints of the name Gobbán, including St Gobbán of Killamery, Co. Kilkenny, whose Feast Day is December 6th. The English form is simply *Gobban*.

GOBNAT, GOBNAIT *f*

This is a feminine form of *Gobban* whose most notable bearer was St Gobnat of Ballyvourney, Co. Cork. She was instructed by an angel to travel through the country until she encountered nine white deer; this would indicate the spot where she was to found her major monastery. She carried out her instructions, founding monasteries on the way, until she encountered her nine white deer at Ballyvourney. She is reputed to have protected Ballyvourney from the plague by prayer and to have protected it from cattle-raiders by the miraculous use of a swarm of bees. She is, understandably, known as the patroness of bees. Her Feast Day is February 11th and *Gobnet* is the most appropriate English form.

GODFREY *see* GODFRITH

GODFRITH, GOTHFRITH, GOFFRAIDH, GOFRAÍ *m*

A borrowing through Old Norse of the Old German name *Godafrid*. It was brought into Ireland by the Vikings, among whom it was popular; it was adopted by the Irish. An incident in 950 shows off the prowess of one Gothfrith: 'Gothfrith son of Sitric, with the Foreigners of Dublin, plundered Kells, and Donaghpatrick, and Ardbreccan, and Dulane, and Kilskeer, and other churches besides; on which occasion three thousand men, or more, were captured, together with a great booty of cows and horses, of gold and silver.' Divine retribution was not long to wait, however; at the close of the year there was 'a great leprosy upon the Foreigners of Dublin, and a bloody flux'. In about 1880, strangely, the last bearer of the name in Maghera, Co. Derry, one Gofraidh Mac Cionnaith, left a death-bed curse on any of his race who should revive the name. The natural English form is *Godfrey*.

GORMÁN *m & f*

Means 'dark' or 'swarthy'. In 769 Gormán, daughter of Flann, son of Áedh, died; in 821 Gormán mac Airtri, king of Munster died. References are not abundant. The English form would be simply *Gorman* for either sex.

GORMLAITH *f*

Means either 'blue princess' or 'illustrious princess'. It was a very popular girl's name in early Ireland, mainly, of course, among princesses. One celebrated Gormlaith, herself the daughter of a king, Flann Sinna, High King of Ireland from 879 to 916, started off her career as the queen of Cormac mac Cuilenáinn, bishop-king of Cashel, until he was beheaded at the battle of Ballaughmoon in 908 — though this marriage is thought to have been purely symbolic, with the ascetic Cormac preserving his virginity. She then married Cormac's enemy — who had actually killed him — Cerball, king of Leinster who, in his turn, was killed in an accident in Kildare in 909. Her third regal spouse was Niall Glúndub, also a king and possibly the half-brother of Gormlaith's father, who was slain in battle against King Sitric, at Dublin, in 919. According to contemporary annals she survived her third husband by nearly thirty years and died 'in penitence' in 948. The best English form is *Gormley*.

GORMLEY see GORMLAITH

GRACE see GRÁINNE

GRÁINNE f

There are two interpretations of this name: one is that it could mean 'she who inspires terror', the other is that it is related to the word *grán* (grain) and applies, therefore, to an ancient corn-goddess. The best known owner of the name is the Gráinne who was betrothed to Finn mac Cumall and is, in consequence, the heroine of the *Pursuit of Diarmaid and Gráinne*. She persuaded Diarmaid, by guile, to elope with her, and thereby save her from an 'arranged' marriage to an older man. Because Diarmaid was an honourable man he deliberately left clues as to where they had spent the night — but always clues that suggested that he had not succumbed to Gráinne's charms, such as pieces of intact bread, raw salmon. Gráinne, however, was determined that the bread should be broken, the salmon cooked; eventually she broke down Diarmaid's resistance and the pursuit, now, at least, more satisfactory from the point of view of Gráinne and Diarmaid, continued for sixteen years. (In memory of the 'circuit of Ireland' involved, megalithic tombs throughout the country are named *Diarmaid and Gráinne's Bed*). Eventually, through the intercession of Aonghus Óg, abetted by Gráinne's father, Cormac mac Airt, Finn mac Cumall was persuaded to set aside his jealousy and anger. Diarmaid and Gráinne settled down at Rath Gráinne, where Diarmaid begot of Gráinne four sons and a daughter. Destiny, however, had to be fulfilled: Diarmaid was killed by a magic boar and Gráinne was eventually reconciled with Finn, although forever disdained by the Fianna. *Gráinne* has no connection with *Grace* apart from the fact that the first three letters are the same — and if any concession has to be made it should be restricted to *Grania*, as a latinised form universally acceptable.

GRANIA see GRÁINNE

GRIAN *f*

Means 'sun' or 'sun-goddess'; near Pallas Green (*Pailis Greine*), in Co. Limerick is Cnoc Greine, the supposed Otherworld seat of Grian, the sun-goddess, who in legend was described as a daughter of Finn. The English form would be simply *Grian*.

GUAIRE *m*

With the meaning 'noble' or 'proud' this was a fairly common name in early Ireland. For one instance Guaire, son of Dúngalach, an O'Brien king, died in 787; for another, at the battle of Carn-Conaill in 648, Guaire Aidhne fled and Diarmait, son of Áedh Slane, was victor. There is, however, a sequel to this. As a result of his defeat Guaire had to make submission to Diarmait 'at the spear's point': he had to lie on his back with the point of the spear in his mouth, while Diarmait put him to the test. 'Now we will learn whether it is for God's sake or vainglory that Guaire practises his notorious alms-giving,' said Diarmait. A beggar came up and asked for alms; Guaire gave him a bodkin of gold, for other wealth he had none. Diarmait's men instantly relieved him of it so the beggar came back; Guaire's heart yearned with pity, so he gave the beggar his well-adorned belt; again Diarmait's men relieved him of it. The beggar came back again and Guaire wept for the sake of the beggar, not for himself. Diarmait bade Guaire rise: 'Thou art vassal to a king that is worthier than I; to the king, I say, of Heaven and of Earth; I will not use dominion over thee.' And so Guaire won his reputation as the paragon of generosity. There is no accepted English form.

HUGH *see* ÁED

IARLAITH, IARLAITHE *m*

The most notable bearer of this name is St Iarlaith, patron of the diocese of Tuam. He was born at Tuam, received his early training with Benignus, who was to be Patrick's chosen successor at Armagh, and was ordained in 468. He returned to Galway and founded his first monastery at a place called *Cluanfois* (Cloonfush, two and a half miles west of Tuam), where he also established a school. Among his pupils were St Brendan of Clonfert and St Colman of Cloyne. He was remarkable for his penitential works and constant prayer; he is said to have performed 300 pious genuflections every day — and a further 300 every night. Becoming increasingly infirm as he grew older he asked St Brendan where would be a good place for him to end his days. Brendan took him in a chariot whose wheels broke at Tuam, thus indicating the appropriate place. Here he founded a second monastery in which he did indeed end his days. His remains are buried in *Teampall na Scríne* on the site of his monastery. The English form of his name is *Jarlath*.

IBOR, IOBHAR *m*

Derived from the word *iobar* (yew-tree); its most famous bearer was St Ibor of Beggerin Island, who is described as one of the most obdurate opponents of St Patrick's mission. (It has been suggested that the main reason for his opposition to St Patrick was that he was a foreigner.) There is an interesting story that under the latinised name, *Abaris*, with the added epithet ' The Hyperborean', he travelled from a northern country to visit Greece. 'Though he appeared a barbarian in dress, yet he spoke Greek with so much facility and correctness that he might be supposed to be an orator from the midst of the Lyceum.' He is said to have been given to divination and to have delivered oracular statements in those countries through which he passed. He had established a pre-Patrician church on Beggerin Island, Co. Wexford (also known as *Inis Iboir*), where there was until recently considerable devotion to him; pilgrims still visit the site of his early church — where, indeed, he was visited by many of his contemporary holy men and women. His Feast Day is April 23rd. Possible forms in English are Ivor or Ivar.

IDA *see* ÍTE

ÍMAR, ÍOMHAR *m*

A borrowing of the Old Norse name Ivarr which was quite popular among the Norse in Ireland and was readily adopted by the Irish — albeit in exchange for Irish names, as the following incidents show. In the year 981 Kildare was plundered by Imhar of Waterford; in the following year, 982, there was a 'battle-rout' by Máelsechlainn, son of Domnall, over Domnall Cloen, king of Leinster and over Ímhar of Waterford, where a great number perished by drowning and killing, including Gilla-Patraic, son of Ímhar. One of the best known Irish bearers of the name was St Ímhar úa hÁedagáin, who was abbot of Armagh from the beginning of the twelfth century, and of whom St Máel m'Áedhóg Ó Morgair (St Malachy) was a disciple. He died on a pilgrimage to Rome in 1134; his Feast Day is April 13th. The best English form would be Ivar.

ITA *see* ITÉ

ÍTE, ÍDE *f*

Means literally 'the act of eating, devouring'; it was the name adopted by a saintly girl, originally, apparently, named Deirdre, born in Co. Waterford about 480, as a punning reference to her 'hunger for Divine Love'. When she arrived at marriageable age her father proposed that she marry a noble youth; as a result of her prayers an angel appeared to her father and succeeded in persuading him to permit her to take up the religious life, by declaring that 'in another part of the country shall she serve our Lord, and become Patron over the race that inhabits it'. Accordingly she set off to find a place to found her monastery.

Pious women flocked to join her and a local land-owner offered her some land adjoining her monastery; she accepted only four acres — sufficient for no more than a vegetable-garden. The place where she founded her monastery was to be known as Killeedy ('Ita's Church'), Co. Limerick. She herself was given to regular, rigorous — indeed excessive — fasting, and was endowed with miraculous powers of healing. Breandán of Clonfert is only one of the saints who are said to have received their early education at her school. She has been called 'Foster Mother of the Irish Saints' and is recognised as Patroness of the Parish of Killeedy. She died at Killeedy in 570 and her grave is at the junction of the nave and chancel of the Romanesque church. Her Feast Day is January 15th. The usual anglicised form of her name is Ita or Ida.

IVAR see IBOR and ÍMAR

IVOR see IBOR

JAMES *see* SÉAMUS

JANE *see* SÍNE *or* SINÉAD

JANET *see* SINÉAD

JARLATH *see* IARLAITH

JOAN *see* SIOBHÁN

JOHN *see* EOIN *or* SEÁN

K

KANE *see* CAHÁN

KARAN/EN *see* CAIRENN

KAREL *see* CAIRELL

KATHERINE *see* CAITRÍONA

KATHLEEN *see* CAITLÍN

KEAN *see* CIAN

KEELIN *see* CÁELFIND

KEEVA *see* CAOIMHE

KELLACH *see* CEALLACH

KELLY *see* CEALLACH

KENNETH *see* CINÁED

KERILL *see* CAIRELL

KEVIN *see* CAOIMHÍN

KIAN *see* CIAN

KIERA *see* CIAR

KIERAN *see* CIARÁN

KILIAN *see* CILLÉNE

LABRAID, LABHRAIDH *m*

Literally means 'speaker'. Labraid Longsech is the legendary ancestor of the Leinstermen of whom a famous story is told, of how the king had ass's ears. The king was extremely secretive about this, and so, whichever poor lad drew the lot of cutting the king's hair lost his life immediately after completing the task. On one occasion this terminal task fell to the only child of a poor widow who, knowing the probable outcome, begged and beseeched the king to spare her only support. The king agreed to suspend sentence on the strict condition that the lad would never divulge what he had seen. The lad gladly agreed and when he saw the ears, pretended there was nothing unto-ward; the burden of secrecy, however, was too much for him, and he wasted away. On the advice of a Druid he divulged his secret to no man, but relieved himself of his burden in the open air, near a willow tree. It soon happened that the harp of Craftíne, the king's harpist, needed fixing; to make a new instrument he used the very willow near which the lad had told his story: the harp would play only one song: 'Labraid Longsech has the ears of an ass'; the king repented of his cruelty and thereafter displayed his ears openly. The name might be rendered in English as Lowry.

LABRÁS, LABHRÁS *m*

Literally means 'a laurel bush'; it would, therefore, be a better equivalent for Laurence than is Lorcán; indeed in the notice of the death of 'Laurence' O'Toole in the fragment preserved of McCarthy's book he is described as Labhrás. Laurence would seem an acceptable English form.

LÁEGAIRE, LAOGHAIRE *m*

It has been suggested that its probable meaning is 'calf-herd'. There are several saints of the name, one of whom is St Láegaire of Lough Conn, whose Feast Day is May 11th. It was also the name of several kings and princes, one of whom was Láegaire, son of Niall, during whose reign St Patrick, in 432, arrived in Ireland. This Láegaire died in 461 — in the same year to which some sources ascribe the death of St Patrick. He had two wives, Feidlim the long-haired and Aeife the daughter of Ailell. Another Láegaire, who died in 812, was son of Cugamma and king of the Cinell-Coirpri. The name, of course, is also enshrined in the name of Dún Laoghaire, Co. Dublin. The most obvious English form would be *Leary*.

LAISRÉAN, LAISRÉN *m*

A diminutive form of *laisre* (flame). Among the several saints of the name is St Laisrén of Devenish, Co. Fermanagh (more commonly known by his pet-name, Molaisse) He studied under Finnian of Clonard; one day he was sitting in the shade of some trees with a colleague called Mogue, discussing whether they should work together or separately; the tree under which Mogue was sitting fell, pointing south; the tree under which Laisrén was sitting fell, pointing north. They recognised the divine indication and tearfully bade each other farewell. Mogue went south to found his monastery at Ferns, Laisrén went north to found his at Devenish. He is said to have made a pilgrimage to Rome and to have brought several relics back to Ireland. His Feast Day is September 12th; there is no real English equivalent, but *Laisren* or even the pet-form, *Molaisse*, would be most suitable.

LAOISE *f*

Possibly this name is the same as *Luigsech*, a name derived from the name of the god Lug, which means 'radiant girl'. There is a St Luigsech, or Laoise, whose Feast Day is May 22nd. While it has been equated with *Lucy* there is no connection. It is best left as *Laoise*.

LASAIRFHÍONA, LASAIRÍONA *f*

Is a compound of *lasair* (flame) and *fíon* (wine). It was quite a popular name with the O'Conors, as for example Lasairfhíona, daughter of Cathal Crovderg O'Conor, wife of Domnall Mór

O'Donnell and mother of Domnall Beg, 'head of the women of Leth-Cuinn', who died in 1282. Indeed in 1381 the deaths in the one year of two ladies of the name are recorded: Lasairfhíona daughter of Turlough O'Conor and wife of Mac Raghnail, and Lasairfhíona, daughter of Fergal O'Duigenan and wife of O'Meehin of Ballagh. The name is commonly anglicised *Lassarina* or *Lasrina*; the name *Fíona*, which has been unfairly accused of not being a genuine Irish name, but an invention by William Sharp for his fictional character Fiona Macleod, is often used as a shortened form of *Lasairfhíona*.

LASSARINA *see* LASAIRFHÍONA

LAURENCE *see* LABRÁS *and* LORCAN

LEARY *see* LÁEGAIRE

LENNÁN, LEANNÁN *m*

This name means 'lover, sweetheart' and was most in use among the families of Co. Clare. Lennán mac Cathrannach was king of Corcu Baiscinn from 898 until his death in 915. The most straightforward English form is *Lennan*.

LÍADAN, LÍADAIN *f*

Possibly simply means 'grey lady'. It was the name of the tragic heroine of a 'Heloise and Abelard' situation. Líadan was a poetess, her lover, another poet, was Cuirithir; for some reason Líadan spurned him and became a nun; in despair Cuirithir also espoused the monastic life instead of his beloved Líadan. Both, of course, regretted their folly; Cuirithir was sent away from Ireland; heart-broken Líadan died of grief at a stone where Cuirithir had been wont to pray, having expressed her grief at her actions: 'Cen áinius/in gním í do-rigénus/an ro-carus ro-cráidius' (No pleasure/that deed I did, tormenting him/tormenting what I treasure). *Liadan* seems the most appropriate English form.

LIAM *see* **UILLIAM**

LOMMÁN, LOMÁN *m*

Is derived from the word *lomm* (bare). There are several saints of the name, of whom St Lommán of Trim, Co. Meath, is probably the best known. According to ancient tradition the lord of the district, Fedelmid, son of King Láegaire of Tara (during whose reign St Patrick arrived in Ireland) presented 'his territory with all his goods and all his race' to Patrick and Lommán, who is supposed to have been a nephew. Patrick founded a church at Trim, and Lommán was its first bishop. For generations after, the successors of Lommán were chosen exclusively from the descendants of Fedelmid. St Lommán's Feast Day is October 11th; the received English form is *Loman*.

LONÁN *m*

This name is a derived diminutive from *lon* (blackbird). There are several saints of the name, including St Lonán Finn whose Feast Day is January 22nd, and about whom nothing else is known. There is even a St Lon, whose Feast Day is June 24th. The English form is simply *Lonan*.

LORCÁN, LORCCÁN *m*

Derived from *lorcc* (cruel or fierce). Its best known bearer was St Lorcán Ó Tuathail (anglicised as 'Laurence' O'Toole), who was born in Leinster and studied at the monastery of Glendalough, Co. Wicklow, where he became a member of the community and, in 1153, Abbot; during his abbacy he founded the Augustinian Priory of St Saviour. In 1162 he became Archbishop of Dublin and introduced the Augustinian rule to Christchurch Cathedral. Having at first resisted the Frankish, or Anglo-Norman, conquest of Ireland, when Henry II of England arrived in person in 1171, equipped with papal authority, Lorcán submitted to him. In 1179 he was summoned by Pope Alexander III to the Third Lateran Council in Rome; in return for permission to travel through England, King Henry extracted from him a promise to do nothing 'prejudicial to the King or his Kingdom'.

Lorcán was appointed Papal Legate and supplied with bulls guaranteeing Papal protection for all the rights of his Church. He went to England again in 1180 as an intermediary between Ruaidhrí Úa Conchobair and Henry, who, because of his displeasure at the content of the bulls, prevented Lorcán's return to Ireland. Henry went to Normandy, Lorcán followed him; before the King agreed to meet him he died at the Augustinian monastery of Eu, in France, in 1180. His Feast Day, the anniversary of his death, is November 14th; he was canonised by Pope Honorius III, in 1226, one of the three Irish saints to be so recognised. The best English form of the name is *Lorcan*; it has no connection whatever with the Latin-derived *Laurence*.

LOWRY *see* LABRAID

MÁEL COLUIM, MAOLCHOLUIM *m*

Means 'servant of Colm' or 'devotee of Colm'. As a name it was more popular in Scotland, where indeed it was a name borne by several kings, presumably because of Colm's mission. Possibly because of his family connections it was used in Donegal as well, an example being Máelcoluim úa Canannáin, king of Cinél-Conall, who died in 956. It is regularly anglicised as *Malcolm*.

MÁEL ÍOSU, MAOL ÍOSA *m*

Means 'devotee of Christ', a name which spread from clerical into lay usage. Important clerical bearers of the name included abbots of Armagh and Inis Cathaig. The best known Máel Ísu, however, was Máel Ísu úa Brolcháin, a religious lyric poet who died in 1086. Many of his best-known poems are on the theme 'lead us not into temptation' as summed up in his 'Lord guard me', with its all-embracing last stanza 'Let me fall into none of the well-known great eight chief sins: O Christ, come to me, to chase them and quell them.' A reasonable English form would be *Maeliosa*, though *Melisa* has been used.

MAEVE *see* MEDB

MÁIRE *f*

A borrowing of the name *Maria*. In the early period the name of the Virgin Mary was considered too sacred to be used as a personal name. In the later medieval period, however, in place of the compounds such as *Máel Muire* (devotee of Mary) which had been used, the form *Muire* was reserved for the Virgin while the form *Máire* was used as a personal name and became relatively common. In 1532, for example, Máire, daughter of Mac Sweeny Fanad, and wife of O'Boyle, died suddenly, after having been thrown from her horse at the door of her own house. In 1561 Máire, daughter of Calvagh, son of Manus, son of Aodh Dubh O'Donnell, died of horror, loathing, grief and deep anguish in consequence of the severity of the imprisonment inflicted on her father, Calvagh, by O'Neill, in her presence. Among the distinguished bearers of the name was Máire ní Scolai, born in Dublin in 1909. She went to Galway, where she appeared in Mícheál Mac Liammóir's *Diarmaid agus Gráinne*. She became widely known for her collecting, interpretation and performance of traditional Irish songs. She died in Galway in 1985. While *Mary* is the obvious English form, *Maura* and *Moira* are used as well; the Irish diminutive *Máirín* has generated the English name *Maureen*.

MÁIRÉAD f

Is either a by-form of *Margreg* (Margareta) or more probably is a diminutive of *Máire* (Maria). There is no real English equivalent.

MALACHI, MALAICI m

A name borrowed from the last of the 'Twelve Minor Prophets' of the Old Testament, meaning 'My Messenger'. It became particularly associated with Ireland as a result of its adoption by its most eminent bearer, Máel Maedhóg Ó Morgair. He was born in 1094 or 1095 at Armagh; his father died when he was eight years of age and he was placed under the care of a hermit, Ímar úa hÁedagáin; he was ordained as a priest at the age of twenty-five by St Cellach, for whom he served as vicar from 1119 to 1121. After further training at Lismore he was appointed Bishop of Down and Connor, and finally, in 1134, the Irish Annals were able to record 'Máel Máedhóc Ó Morgair do dul a comorbus Pádraic la guidhe fear nEireann' (Maol Maedhóg Ó Morgair entered into the succession of Patrick with the prayers of the men of Ireland). In 1137 he retired from his See and later made his first visit to Rome, passing through Clairvaux on the way; he and St Bernard became fast friends and as a result of this friendship the first Cistercian monastery in Ireland opened in 1142 at Mellifont, Co. Louth, soon to be followed by others. Malachy returned from Rome as Papal Legate, and was instructed by the Pope to convene a Council of Bishops. This did not take place until 1148; on his way to Rome to acquire the palls for the archbishoprics of Armagh and Cashel, Malachy died at Clairvaux on November 1st/2nd. St Bernard shortly wrote a biography of Malachy in which he recorded for posterity Malachy's great achievements in reforming the Church in Ireland, bringing it into greater contact and conformity with the Church in Rome and Europe. In 1190 he was canonised by Pope Clement III — the first Irish saint to be so recognised. His Feast Day is November 3rd. The English form of *Malachi* is simply *Malachy*.

MALCOLM *see* MÁEL COLUIM

MAREN *see* MUIREANN

MARGARET *see* MÁRGRÉG

MÁRGRÉG, MÁIRGRÉG, MÁIRGHRÉAD f
This is a form of the Latin *Margareta*, a name made popular in Scotland as a result of the marriage of Malcolm III of Scotland to exiled Margareta, who had been reared to the age of twelve in the Hungarian Court. She was later to become St Margaret. Its popularity spread to Ireland, and, from the fourteenth century on, it was quite common. One of the most interesting owners of the name was Máirgrég, wife of Calbach Úa Conchobuir, king of Úi Failge. She and Calbach hosted a great traditional feasting of court-poets and historians at Killeigh, Co. Offaly, in 1451. Máirgrég is described as 'standing on the garrets of the great church, clad in cloth of gold with her dearest friends about her, her clergy and judges'; meanwhile Calbach greeted the learned and artistic throng. As well as feasting the intellectuals, Máirgrég fed the hungry and clad the orphans. The most fascinating comment on the interests and talents of Máirgrég is that she was the only woman interested 'in preparing highways and erecting bridges and churches and making Mass-books'. The English form of the name is, of course, *Margaret*.

MARTAN, MÁIRTÍN m

A name which became popular in Ireland as a result of the wide-spread devotion to the fourth-century Martin of Tours. A Martan, who was abbot of both Clonmacnoise, Co. Offaly, and Devenish, Co. Fermanagh, 'fell asleep' in 868, while in 915 Martain, bishop of Roscommon, died. The Latin form, *Martinus*, was used for the Feast of St Martin (November 11th), in 891. *Máirtín* is the form in use today; *Martin* is, of course, the English form.

MARTIN *see* MARTAN

MARY *see* MÁIRE

MAURA *see* MÁIRE

MAUREEN *see* MÁIRE

MEDB, MEADHBH, MÉABH f

The meaning is 'intoxicating, she who makes men drunk'. She was queen of Connacht and wife to, among others, Ailill, with whom she was associated in the famous epic *Táin Bó Cuailnge*. Perhaps the best description of her is her own. 'My father was in the high-kingship of Ireland, namely Eochu mac Find meic Findomain . . . He had six daughters . . . I was the noblest and worthiest of them. I was the most generous of them in bounty and the bestowal of gifts. I was best of them in battle and fight and combat . . . I was never without one man in the shadow of another.' The climax of this conversation between Medb and Ailill (known as 'The pillow talk') was a comparison of their possessions and the discovery that lacking from Medb's was a bull the equal of Ailill's. This, in its turn, led to the desperate attempts on the part of Medb and Ailill to acquire the bull known as the Donn Cuailnge (the brown bull of Cooley) and the events described in the famous epic. There is a common Irish diminutive form, *Meidhbhín*; the received English form is *Maeve*.

MEL *m*
No explanation of the meaning of this name appears to be available. By far the most famous bearer of it was St Mel, bishop and patron of Ardagh, Co. Limerick. He was a nephew of St Patrick, his mother being Darerca, Patrick's sister. He established a monastery at Ardagh. He had predicted the future greatness and sanctity of St Brigit while she was still in the womb, and later confirmed her and bestowed upon her the veil. While he was at Ardagh rumours reached Patrick of a possible clandestine relationship between Mel and another sister of Patrick, Lupita, Mel's own aunt, who was staying in the monastery of Ardagh. While, apparently, finding Mel and Lupita innocent of any illicit relationship, Patrick was led to issue a decree that 'consecrated men and women — even although nearly related — should live apart, and in separate habitations, lest the weak might be scandalised, or that any injury might be inflicted on religious decorum, by the existence of possible causes leading to temptation'. Mel is believed to have written down the acts, virtues and miracles of his uncle, Patrick, while Patrick was still alive. Mel died in 487; his Feast Day is February 6th; the English form of his name is simply M*el*.

MELISA *see* MÁEL ÍOSU

MELLÁN, MEALLÁN *m*
This name is derived from an early word for 'lightning'. There are several early saints who bore it. One of them was in a party of six Irish clerical students who encountered St Patrick in the course of his journey to or from Rome. They knelt before him and asked his blessing; he happily gave it and predicted that all six would one day become bishops — and also presented them with a skin, on which he was wont to stand while preaching, to serve as a satchel for their books. In due course St Mellán founded his church at Kilrush, Co. Westmeath and fulfilled Patrick's prophecy by becoming a bishop. His Feast Day is

January 28th; an English form for the name would be simply *Mellan*.

MÍCHEÁL, MÍCHÉL m

A borrowing of the biblical name of one of the archangels. It is only comparatively recently that it has become very popular in Ireland. One of its most distinguished bearers was Mícheál Mac Liammóir, born in Cork in 1899, most renowned as an actor and writer. In 1928 his *Diarmaid agus Gráinne* was performed at the opening of Taibhdhearc na Gaillimhe. In 1928 he and Hilton Edwards launched the Gate Theatre which brought to Dublin most of the major European plays of the time, while many notable Irish plays had their first production there. His own creative output was prodigious, including ten plays. His ideal was the worthy one of an Ireland Gaelic and European rather than Anglo-American. He died, the recipient of many deserved honours, in 1978. The English equivalent is, of course, *Michael*.

MIREN *see* MUIREANN *or* MUIRGEN

MOIRA *see* MÁIRE

MOLAISSE *see* LAISRÉAN

MONA *see* MUADNAT

MONINNE, MONINNA f

Another name for Blinne, of Killevy, Co. Armagh; through her intercession it is related that a mute poet reacquired the power of speech and his first halting utterance was 'Ninne, Ninne', which is said to account for her name. At one stage she worked with St Brigit for a while, serving as the portress in the hospital maintained at Kildare. She was endowed with a gift of healing the infirm and the possessed. Her reputation as a bene-factress to the poor caused them to flock to her door; they always departed laden with bounty, to such an extent that her nuns complained that they were left with little or nothing. After her sojourn with Brigit she returned to the North and established her community at Killevy, Co. Armagh, on the foot of Slieve Gullion. Here again her generosity to the needy left her community short of supplies. Her Feast Day is July 6th. The best English form of the name is *Moninna*.

MÓR *f*
The name means 'tall' or 'great' and was extremely popular in later medieval Ireland. An early bearer of the name, Mór-Mumhan, daughter of Áedh Bennan and wife to Finghin, king of Munster, died in 631. She is described as the paragon of the Irish women of her time. Another Mór, daughter of Mac Caba, who died in 1527, was described as 'the nurse of the learned and destitute of Ireland'. It seems to have been used as a substitute for *Máire*, to avoid using the name of the Mother of God as a personal name, and, in consequence, to have become rather confused with it. There is a diminutive form, *Móirín*, which is so close to the diminutive, *Máirín*, of *Máire*, as to be rendered into English as *Moreen*, or even *Maureen*.

MOREEN *see* MÓR

MUADNAT, MUADHNAIT *f*
This name is derived from the word *muad* (noble, good). The best known saintly bearer of the name is St Muadhnat, reputed to be a sister of St Molaisse of Devenish, who founded a monastery near that of St Fintan at Drumcliffe, Co. Sligo. Her Feast Day is January 6th. The received English forms of her name are *Monat* and *Mona*.

MUIREANN, MAIRENN *f*
Possibly the meaning is 'sea-white' or 'sea-fair'. This was the name of the wife of a king of Connacht, Raghallach mac Fuatach.

Out of jealousy and by guile — 'he was self-willed and full of malice' — he slew his own nephew. A sooth-sayer told Mairenn that 'a king who hath slaughtered all his own brethren, by his own issue shall the downfall of such a one be wrought', and that as far as she herself was concerned 'by thine own womb's fruit thou shalt be undone'. At the time Mairenn was pregnant and so, in the light of the prophecy they decided the infant should be done to death; a daughter was born and handed over to a swineherd for killing. The swineherd, revolted at the thought of killing the child, left the babe to the care of a pious woman, who reared the child until she was the fairest woman in the whole of Ireland. When Raghallach set eyes upon her, not realising she was his daughter, he became totally besotted. Many saints, including Feichín of Fore, aghast at the situation, fasted upon him and prayed that 'by weapons of dishonour he should perish in a foul pit'. And so it came about: Raghallach was beaten to death by churls with turf-spades. Mairenn herself ended up married to Diarmaid, the High King. *Miren* or *Maren* would be suitable forms in English.

MUIREDACH, MUIREADHACH, MUIRÍOCH *m*

One explanation of this name is that it is possibly derived from *muiredach* (lord, master). It was a name popular among the kings and princes of Ireland, and also among saints. A Muiredach, abbot of Monasterboice, Co. Louth, who died in 922, is commemorated in an inscription on a High Cross there which says 'Oroit do Muiredach Lasndernad in Chros' (a prayer for Muiredach by whom the Cross was made). One interesting bearer of the name was Muiredach Mac Robartaig (whose family, hereditary guardians of the Cathach of St Colmcille, gave their name to Ballymagroarty, Co. Donegal). In 1172 he set off with two companions for Ratisbon in Bavaria. After a year there he was admitted to the order of St Benedict in the monastery of Michelsberg and gained a reputation for great austerity. He was employed by the Abbess Emma at Ratisbon in the transcription of books; an autograph copy of the Epistles of St Paul, in his hand, survived in the Imperial Library in Vienna until the last century at least. He was known in Bavaria as Marianus Scotus. He died in Ratisbon in 1088, where he is buried; his Feast Day is January 9th. The name has been anglicised as *Murry* or *Murray* or even *Murdough*.

MUIRGEL, MUIRGHEAL f

Means 'sea-bright' or 'sea-white'. It was a name borne by a daughter of Máelsechnaill, who was implicated in the slaying of the son of Ausli in 882 and died herself, in old age, in 926. Ironically enough, a Muirgel who was the wife of a swineherd is better known, for she appears in the story *Buile Suibhne* (The Frenzy of Suibhne). It was to St Moling that her husband, Mongán, was swineherd, while she herself served as cook. In his wanderings Suibhne had arrived at Moling's monastery. Moling welcomed him and told that not only was his coming prophesied but also the fact that he would die there. Muirgel was instructed by the saint to leave out milk for Suibhne every evening: accordingly every evening she dug her heel in the cowdung and filled the impression with new milk for Suibhne to drink. Muirgel and another woman had a dispute in which the other woman accused her of preferring Suibhne to her husband; Mongán's sister was listening; she told the story to Mongán; he promptly thrust a spear into poor Suibhne. It has been suggested that the English name *Muriel* is not only an acceptable English form but is actually derived from *Muirgel*.

MUIRGEN, MUIRÍN, MUIRENN f

Means 'born of the sea'. Muirenn, daughter of Congalach, who died in 978, was abbess of Kildare. The best known bearer, whose story consists of an explanation as to how the name came about, was a daughter of Eochaid and Ébhliu, and her name was Líban (Beauty of women). She was one of the three that survived the eruption of Lough Neagh and miraculously preserved in her bower beneath the lough until one day she expressed the wish to take on the shape of a salmon, 'scouring the sea and swimming'; into a salmon she was turned and into an otter her lap-dog was turned, so that he could follow in her wake. For three hundred years she stayed under the sea until one day Béoán, out in a currach, heard a chant as of angels from under the sea. Líban told him her story and, having exacted from her a promise that she would be buried in his church, Béoán arranged to meet her in a year's time. And so, in a year's time the nets were cast and 'she was brought to land, her form and her whole description being wonderful. Numbers came to see her and she in a vessel with water round about her'. She elected to be baptised and go straight to heaven; she was christened 'Muirgen' and was buried at the church of Béoán (or Béoc), on Saints' Island in Lough Derg and 'in that place wonders and miracles are wrought through her and there she (after the manner of every other sainted virgin) enjoys honour and reverence even as God hath bestowed them on her in heaven'. Her Feast Day is January 27th; an acceptable English version would be Miren.

MURCHADH m

This name means 'sea-battler' and was a very popular name in early Ireland. It seems to have been shunned by saints, but it was popular among kings and princes. In 714 not only was Murchadh, son of Diarmait, son of blind Airmedach, king of the Úi Néill, killed, but another Murchadh, son of Bran, king of Leinster, made a hosting to Cashel. In 740 Fergal, king of Ireland, lost his son Murchadh, while in 764 the two sons of Domnall, king of Ireland, who had, himself died in 762, Donnchad and Murchadh, joined issue at the battle of Carn-Fiachach (Carn, Co. Westmeath); Murchadh was slain in the battle. The best English form is probably Murrough.

MURDOCH see MUIREDACH

MURIEL see MUIRGEL

MURR(A)Y *see* MUIREDACH

MURROUGH *see* MURCHADH

NAOMH *f*

The word *naomh* in Irish simply means 'a saint'; it is one of several Irish words that have, in recent years, been usurped from their normal usage and converted into fore-names. There is, it would seem, a precedent for this kind of thing in that the ancient martyrologies (lists of saints) were accused of 'inventing saints out of place-names'. Since it is obviously the name itself that is the attraction there is no point in rendering it *Saint* in English.

NAOISE, NÓISE *m*

Was one of the three sons of Uisliu, the others being Áindle and Ardán. All served Conchobhar mac Nessa, the king of the Ulaidh, reigning at Emhain Macha (Navan, Co. Armagh). Naoise, however, had been observed by Deirdre, the beautiful young maiden the king was rearing in order to have her as his wife, and she had noted that he conformed to her prescription of the man she wanted: 'hair the colour of a raven's wing, cheeks the colour of fresh blood, and skin as white as snow'. She obliged him to elope with her, his brothers coming too. At first they stayed in Ireland, but Conchobhar kept hounding them and eventually drove them out of Ireland. They went to Scotland where they settled in the wilderness; when the wild game of the mountains was exhausted they stole cattle, until the men of Scotland went after them. The king of Scotland intervened and took them into his employ as mercenaries, he, too, falling victim to the charms of Deirdre. Eventually they had to leave Scotland and were lured back to Ulster by promises of safety from Conchobhar; and false promises they turned out to be, for no sooner had they arrived at Emhain than they were ambushed and all three brothers killed. There is no real English equivalent.

NÁRBFLAITH *f*

This name probably means 'noble princess' and is one of a series of 'princess' names. Slightly irregularly it was the name borne by the wife of an abbot of Trim, Co. Meath, who died in 756. Narvla could be used in English.

NARVLA *see* NÁRBFLAITH

NEILL *see* NIALL

NESS, NEAS, NESSA *f*

There seems to be no ready interpretation of this name. She was the daughter of Eochaidh Salbuide and wife of Fachtna, king of Ulster. According to one legend she had a child by Cathbad the magician, who was to be called Conchobhar mac Nessa. Her husband Fachtna died, and after his death his half-brother, Fergus mac Róich, succeeded him as king. Fergus had fallen in love with Nessa and pressed her to marry him; she agreed only on condition that he permit her son Conchobhar to rule for a year in his place. Reluctantly Fergus agreed; by the end of the year, with the astute help of Nessa, Conchobhar had conducted his kingship so skilfully that even Fergus had to concede that he was an exceptional king. This is one explanation of why Fergus and his followers went into exile in Connacht, taking service with Medb and Ailill, placing Fergus on the other side when the war described in *Táin Bó Cuailnge* broke out between the Ulstermen and the men of Ireland. Nessa is the best English form.

NIALL *m*

There is a certain amount of disagreement about the meaning of this name: some authorities connect it with *nel* (cloud), others hold that it means 'passionate' or 'vehement'. The most famous bearer of the name was, of course, the legendary Niall Naígiallach (Niall of the Nine Hostages). The choosing of Niall to succeed his father as king, over his four brothers, was cunningly conceived by Sithchenn, the smith who dwelt in Tara, who was also a seer of wondrous capacity. He lured them into the forge and then set fire to it: Niall won the test, for it was he who brought out the anvil. Neill is the accepted anglicised form though Niall is regularly also used.

NIAMH, NIAM f

With the meaning 'brightness, lustre, radiance' this name might seem appropriate for the model of the *femme fatale* in Irish mythology. One Niamh was daughter of Celtchair mac Cuthacair and was married off by him to Conganchas mac Daire — who had the gift of invincibility, no weapon could harm him — for the sole purpose of finding his weak spot so that Celtchair might slay him. She shortly discovered that he could be slain only by having spears penetrating the soles of his feet and the calves of his legs. She duly reported this back to her father, who, in his turn, duly slew Conganchas. Another of the same name was Niamh Chinn Óir (Niamh of the golden head), who, in a 'Christianised' tale, seduced Oisín and bore him off on her horse to the Land of Promise, where they had several children, including Oscar and Fionn. Eventually Oisín began to pine for Ireland; when he did return, on the magic horse she had provided (and from which she had warned him not to dismount), he found that three hundred years had passed, and, falling off the horse by accident, he was turned instantly from a handsome youth into a blind and withered old man. There is no specifically English form.

NORA *see* ONÓRA

NOREEN *see* ONÓRA

NUALA *see* FIONNUALA

ODARNAT, ODHARNAIT, ÓRNAIT f

This name is the version for females of *Odhrán* and so it means either 'a sallow female' or is simply a female name derived from the old word for an otter. There is a virgin saint with the name of whom virtually nothing is known except that her Feast Day is November 13th. Anglicised versions are *Ornat* or *Orna*,

ODRÁN, ODHRÁN, ÓRÁN m

This name may be derived from *odhar* meaning 'dun-coloured, sallow'; another suggestion is that it is derived from an old name of the otter. There are nearly a score of saints of this name, including Odhrán of Latteragh, Co Tipperary. Perhaps the most deserving bearer of the name, however, is Odhrán who was charioteer to St Patrick. When Patrick was on his mission in Munster, a local chieftain, Failge Berraide, decide to assassinate the apostle; Odhrán got wind of the plot and persuaded Patrick to change places with him and drive the chariot himself, pleading that he was exhausted. Patrick complied and so, when Failge leapt out of his ambush, it was poor Odhrán that was transfixed by his spear. Despite Odhrán's pleas, the assassin was instantly struck down. The best English form is *Oran*.

ÓENGUS, ÁENGUS, AONGHUS m

With a meaning, presumably, of something like 'sole strength', it was a name common to a number of legendary heroes, such as Óengus Gaí Buaibthech (of the terrible spear) who killed Ceallach with a spear in revenge for the rape of his niece; of historical kings and princes, such as Óengus, son of Suibhne, king of Mourne, who was killed by Garfhidh, son of Máelbrigte, in 849; of gods, even, such as Aonghus Óg, the god of love; and, of course, of saints. Of these the best known is Óengus Céile Dé, truly a saint and a scholar, and a great reformer of the early Irish Church. Even as a youth he was given to extreme forms of asceticism, reciting the entire Psalter every day, part of it while tied by his neck to a stake, immersed to the waist in cold water. He occupied a solitary cell at a place called Dysert (hermitage), near Stradbally, Co. Laois, before joining the community at Clonenagh, Co. Laois. It was here that he began his celebrated martyrology, the *Feilire of Óengus*, which he actually completed at Tallaght, Co. Dublin. As well as being a saint and a scholar he was a noted poet; in one of his poems, A *Prayer for Forgiveness*, he says: 'I am repentant, Lord, for my transgression, as is right: Christ of thy mercy, forgive me every sin that may be attributed to me.' His Feast Day is March 11th; the normal English version of his name is *Angus*.

OISÍN, OISSÍNE *m*

This name is a diminutive form of *os* (deer or stag); while it is the name of four or five saints, its best known owner was the son of Finn mac Cumall and Sadb. Sadb had been turned into a deer and in that form she had reared their child, which was why Oisín got his name. Oisín was highly susceptible to the charms of women; in addition to his wife, Éibhir, and his three-hundred year dalliance with Niamh Chinn Óir, his relationship with another Niamh was to cost his father Finn and the Fianna dear. This Niamh was the daughter of Áengus Tírech, king of Munster. She and Oisín had travelled all the way to Moira, in Co. Down, where they spent six weeks together, at a pool later called 'the well of women'. Her father summoned all the men of Munster and pursued them. Niamh caught sight of them; out of sheer shame she expired on the spot, 'her heart as a lump of black blood passed from her mouth'. When Áengus saw his dead daughter he was even more annoyed and challenged Finn and the Fianna to battle. The Fianna convinced Finn that he would not have right on his side if he fought the king of Munster over his dead daughter and it was agreed that compensation should be paid, which amounted to her own weight in gold and again her own weight in silver. An acceptable English form of the name is *Ossian*, though *Oisin* is increasingly used even in English.

ONÓRA *f*

This is a borrowing of the name *Honora*, popular among the Anglo-Normans and derived probably from the Latin *Honor* (honour, reputation). It was in fairly common use in medieval Ireland and was particularly popular among the O'Briens, no less than three O'Brien daughters recorded as bearing the name between 1579 and 1600. An Onorina (a diminutive form) Brenach (Walsh) has the distinction of being commemorated, with her husband Sir John Grace, Baron of Courtstown, in a tomb carved by Ruaidhrí O'Tunney, dated 1552, preserved in St Canice's Cathedral, Kilkenny. Oddly enough another tomb in the cathedral commemorates Honorina Shortall. The name gave rise to the forms popular in modern Ireland: *Nóra* and *Nóirín*. The English forms are *Nora* and *Noreen*.

OONAGH *see* ÚNA

ORAN *see* ODHRÁN

ÓRLA, ÓRLAITH *f*

Another of the series of 'princess' names, meaning 'golden princess'. In a prose text based on a poem on famous women by a twelfth-century historian from Fermanagh, which contains the names of over three hundred women, *Órlaith* is the fifth most frequent name, scoring sixteen (while *Sadb*, the most frequent, scores twenty-five). In pre-Norman Ireland it was borne by both a sister and a niece of Brian Boru, the high king, while the unfortunate Tigernán úa Ruairc, king of Breifne, who lost his wife Dervorguilla to Diarmait Mac Murrough, had a daughter called Órlaith. Its popularity had declined but has now increased markedly. *Orla* is the preferred form in English.

ORNA(T) *see* ODARNAT

OSCAR *m*

This name has been interpreted as meaning 'deer-lover'; while it was the name of a grandson of Finn mac Cumall, one of the great warriors of the Finn cycle of tales, there can be little doubt that its most widely known bearer was Oscar Fingal O'Flahertie Wills Wilde, son of the brilliant Sir William Wilde, surgeon and antiquarian. He was born in 1854, in Dublin, and was educated at Portora Royal School, Enniskillen; Trinity College, Dublin; and Magdalen College, Oxford. He was closely associated with the Aesthetic Movement and began his real literary career with the delightful *The Happy Prince and Other Tales* in 1888, followed by his only novel, *The Picture of Dorian Gray*, in 1891. His greatest success was as a playwright, with *Lady Windermere's Fan* (1892), *An Ideal Husband* and *The Importance of Being Earnest* (both in 1895) and *Salome* (1894, in English translation). In 1895, however, after a trial for libel involving Lord Alfred Douglas and his father, The Marquess of Queensbury, he himself was tried for homosexuality and convicted, spending much of his two-year sentence in Reading Gaol; based on his experiences there his *Ballad of Reading Gaol* was published in 1898. He died in Paris in 1900. His apologia, *De Profundis*, was published posthumously in 1905. The English form remains *Oscar*.

OSSIAN *see* OISÍN

OWEN *see* EÓGAN

PÁDRAIG, PÁTRAIG m

A borrowed form of the Latin *Patricius*. Because of the fact that it was the name of the national apostle it was not in use in Ireland as a personal name, except in the form *Gilla Patraic* (servant of Patrick), until long after it had been used by the Anglo-Normans; in fact it has been suggested that only in the last three hundred years has it been in common use. Patrick's mission in Ireland, after the famous incident of the conversion of King Laoghaire and his court at Tara, was a triumphal tour round the country, in the course of which he converted great numbers of other people, many of whom expressed a wish to be ordained for the religious life. He established many churches throughout the country, over some sixty of which he placed bishops, in the majority of places native Irish whom he had consecrated. He performed many miracles and in the course of a forty-day fast on Croagh Patrick in Co. Mayo, after a conversation with the Angel of the Lord, obtained a positive response to his petition that all the Irish would obtain God's clemency; that barbarian invaders would not prevail against the Irish; that on the Day of Judgment no living person would be in Ireland. Summing up the fruits of his missionary activity in Ireland from its beginning in 432 St Patrick said himself:

> Many were reborn in God through me and afterwards confirmed, and clerics were ordained for them everywhere, for a people just coming to the faith, whom the Lord took from the uttermost parts of the earth.

A worthy modern bearer of the name was Pádraig Colum, born in Longford, where his father was master of the workhouse, in 1881. He began writing for the theatre in 1903, when *Broken Soil* was produced, followed in 1910 by *Thomas Muskerry*, the story of a workhouse master. At about this time he wrote his best known lyric, 'She moved through the fair'. He married Mary Maguire and together they moved to the United States, where they both lectured in comparative literature. His *Collected Poems* appeared in 1953. He died in America in 1972 but is buried in Dublin. The English form of *Pádraig* is of course, *Patrick*, and the Feast Day of St Patrick is March 17th.

PATRICK *see* PÁDRAIG

PEADAR *m*

A borrowing of the biblical name *Peter*. The form *Petair* seems to have been in use among early Irish saints, one of whom has his Feast Day on June 4th. One worthy bearer of the name was Peadar Ó Doirnín, born between 1682 and 1685, possibly in Co. Louth, possibly outside Dundalk. He was obliged to leave home and settled at Drumcree, Co. Armagh; his poem on the ancient divisions of Ireland brought him into contact with Arthur Brownlow of Lurgan, then, rather incredibly, the possessor of the *Book of Armagh*. Brownlow employed him as tutor to his children, while he himself hoped thereby to acquire a knowledge of Irish literature. Inevitably after a number of years their different political attitudes put such a strain on the relationship that Ó Doirnín left the Brownlow household, married, and settled as a schoolmaster near Forkhill, Co. Armagh. His poems dealt with nature and politics in the main, but included some humorous verses as well. He died in 1769. The English equivalent is, of course, *Peter*.

PETER *see* PEADAR *and* PIARAS

PHELIM *see* FEDELMID

PIARAS, PERAIS, FERUS *m*

This is another borrowed form of the biblical name *Peter*, but through the Norman French form *Piaras*. It was very popular among Anglo-Norman settlers, including the Daltons. Towards the end of the fourteenth century the son of Perais Dalton was engaged in a number of rather questionable escapades, only to receive a captured castle as a reward. It was still in use among those of Norman descent in the seventeenth century when Piaras Feiritéir was born in about 1600. He had his family seat near Ballyferriter, on the north-west side of Ferriter's Cove. In the rising of 1641 he took the side of the native Irish and successfully attacked and seized Tralee Castle, albeit wounded in the attack. He was the last of the Kerry commanders to submit to the Cromwellians. His promised safe-conduct was, in typical fashion, dishonoured by Brigadier-General Nelson and he was hanged, along with a priest and a bishop, on Martyrs' Hill, Killarney in 1653. As a scholar and poet he was greatly respected by his contemporaries; his courtly love-poems were highly sophisticated. English forms include *Pierce* and *Piers*, though naturally *Peter* would also be correct.

PIERCE *see* PIARAS

PROINNSIAS m
This is borrowed from the name of St Francis of Assissi, whose death, in 1226, is recorded in Irish annals, but in the form *Fronses*. It appears not to have achieved enormous popularity in Ireland until the present day.

RAGHNALL *m*

A name borrowed from Old Norse meaning 'mighty power'. It was the name of many of the Vikings who had settled in Ireland; at the battle of Tara in 850, where Máel Sechnaill the Great, King of Ireland, defeated the Norse of Dublin, among those who were slain on the Norse side was Raghnall mac Amlaíb. As an indication of how intricate relationships, and interminglings of names had become, in 1402 Cathal Ruadh Mac Raghnaill was killed by the family of Máel Sheachlainn mac Raghnaill and Raghnall took the chieftainship after him. Among the Mac Donnells of Co. Antrim the name was very popular, but in the form *Randal*, as in Randalstown, Co. Antrim. The form *Randal* is probably easier for English use.

RANDAL *see* RAGHNALL

RAYMOND *see* RÉMANN

RÉMANN, RÉAMONN *m*

A name borrowed from the Old German compound of *ragan* (counsel) and *mund* (protection). It was introduced to Ireland by the Anglo-Normans and was quite popular in late medieval times. Indeed among the reinforcements for the first force of Anglo-Norman invaders in 1167 was Rémann Reamus Mac Gearailt (Raymond le Gros Fitzgerald), with ten knights and seventy archers; he was a son of the paternal uncle of Robert FitzStephen and Maurice FitzGerald 'according to the books of the Galls'. The modern English form is, of course, *Raymond*.

RÍAN, RÍGÁN, RÍOGHÁN *m*

Almost certainly a diminutive of *ri* (king); there seems to have been a reflux, whereby the name that originally gave the surname *Ryan* has been replaced, as a fore-name, by that form. There is at least one saint who bears the name. In 845 a Rígán, son of Fergus, was slain in a victory over the Connachtmen by the

Foreigners, while in 895 a Rían, son of Bruddai, was slain by the Vikings. The progenitor of the úi Riain is attributed to the tenth century, while in 1103 a Rían, Lord of Idrone, was involved in a slaughter of the úi Ceinnsealaigh. The favoured English form is Ryan, but Rian would also be acceptable.

RIFACH see RÍOMTHACH

RINACH see RÍOGHNACH

RÍOGHNACH, RÍGHNACH, RÍONACH f
It means 'queenly'. It was the name of a daughter of Medabh, son of Ross mac Trithem, who was wife to Niall of the Nine Hostages. She was, therefore, the mother of Laeghaire, Énna, Maine, Eoghan, two Conalls and Cairbre; thus from her and Niall, to whom it had been predicted 'to thine and thy children's forever the kingdom and supreme power shall be', there was descended an impressive line — two of whom, Conall and Eoghan, have left their marks in the names of Irish counties. There were also two Christian saints of the name, one whose Feast Day is December 18th, the other, February 9th. The name, apart from the latinisation as Regina, is best anglicised as Rinach.

RÍOMTHACH, RÍOFACH f
This name was born by one of the five sisters of Léníne (their brother was St Colman of Cloyne, Co. Cork), who founded a church at Killiney, Co. Dublin, in the sixth century. The church was known as Cill Inghean Léinín (the church of the daughters of Léníne) which in turn became Killiney. An acceptable English form would be Rifach.

RODERICK see RUAIDRÍ

RÓIS, RÓISÍN f
It is thought to be derived from the Old German hros (horse), but has been identified with the Latin name Rosa (rose) from very

early times. It was brought into England by the Normans and thence to Ireland. It is probably best known from the Song 'Róisín Dubh' — one of the many Irish poems or songs that can be interpreted on the one hand as simple love songs, on the other as deep-felt expressions of nationalism; in this case Ireland may be viewed as the beautiful woman to whom the song is addressed: 'A Róisín, ná bíodh brón ort, ná cás anois' (Do not be sad, Róisín, do not sigh). Ironically enough Róis, daughter of O'Doherty, was one of those who boarded the ship brought to Lough Swilly in 1607, on which the Earl O'Neill and the Earl O'Donnell were carried into exile. Despite its apparent similarity, and the fact that it has been assumed to have an affinity, it has been argued, perhaps not totally convincingly, especially with regard to the imagery read into such names as *Róisín Dubh*, that the name has nothing to do with the name *Rose* or even the Latin *Rosa*; the diminutive form *Róisín* is more popular than *Róis*.

RÓNÁN *m*

Is derived from *rón* (seal); it is the name of a number of saints and is contained in an ogham inscription on a cross-inscribed stone at Arraglen, Co. Kerry, commemorating 'Rónán the priest, son of Comgán'. The best known Rónán is probably 'Rónán Finn', of Lann Rónán (Magheralin, Co. Down), because of his role in the story of Suibhne Gelt (mad Sweeney). Suibhne had incurred Rónán's anger because Suibhne had thwarted his efforts to make peace between Domhnall the High King and Congal Claen at the Battle of Magh Rath (Moira, Co. Down), by killing one of Rónán's clerics and even attempting to kill the saint himself. Rónán pronounces his curse: 'Mo mallacht for Suibhne,/ rium is mor a chionaidh,/ a fhogha blaith builidh/ dosaith trem chlog creadhail' ('My curse on Suibhne!/ great is his guilt against me,/ his smooth, vigorous dart/ he thrust through my holy bell'). As a result of the curse Suibhne flies, a stark madman, from the battle-field. After many weird adventures he arrives at Tech Moling, where he is welcomed by St Moling, but warned that it was prophesied that he would die there, which, eventually, he does, in the church. The tale ends: 'so far some of the adventures of Suibhne son of Colman Cuar king of Dal Araidhe'. Rónán's Feast Day is May 22nd; the English for his name is *Ronan*. It is a very popular name on the continent of Europe, especially in Britanny.

RORY *see* RUAIDRÍ

ROSE *see* RÓIS

ROWAN *see* RÚADÁN

RÚADÁN, RÚADHÁN, RHODÁN *m*

Derived from the word *rúad* and meaning 'red-haired' it is a name of which the best-known bearer is St Rúadán of Lorrha, Co. Tipperary. While several 'Lives' of Rúadán exist there is little totally reliable information about him. He was, certainly, a disciple of St Finnian of Clonard and founded his monastery at Lorrha, which was later to become one of the foremost monasteries of Munster, in the sixth century. One rather charming story tells of how he saved a fugitive from the king. He hid the fugitive in his cellar, and when the king asked about the whereabouts of his quarry Rúadán was able to answer, more or less truthfully, 'I don't know — unless he's under your feet.' He shared with so many Irish saints the ability to cure lepers. On one occasion a group of twelve arrived at his monastery seeking a cure; Rúadán stuck his staff in the ground from which a well gushed forth; the lepers bathed in the water and were cured forthwith. His Feast Day is April 15th; acceptable English forms are *Ruan* or *Rowan*.

RUAIDRÍ, RUAIDHRÍ, RUAIRÍ *m*

Means 'Great King' or 'Red king'. It was a common name in medieval Ireland, borne by such kings and princes as Ruaidrí,

son of Fáelán, king of all the Leinstermen, who died in 784 or
Ruaidhrí úa Canannáin who, in 946, made a hosting to Slane
and routed the Foreigners of Dublin, killing and drowning
many of them. A very worthy bearer of the name, who left behind
for posterity to enjoy many products of his craft, was the great
sculptor of the Ossory or Kilkenny school, Ruaidrí Ó Tunney, or
'Roricus Ó Tuyne', as he signed himself, who is known to have
practised between 1501 and 1552, with a workshop at Callan,
Co. Kilkenny. At Kilcooly Abbey, in Co. Tipperary, are no less than
three examples of his work, including his earliest signed and
dated work, the tomb of Piers fitz James Óg Butler of
Clonamicklon, with the high effigy relief of an armoured knight
and panels of 'weepers'. In St Canice's Cathedral in Kilkenny
are eight further examples, including the last signed and dated
work of his, the tomb of Sir John Grace, Baron of Courtstown,
and his wife, Onorina Brenach, of 1552. The best anglicised
form of the name is *Rory*, but as a result of the Latin form used
in the inscriptions on his work, *Roderick* is also acceptable.

RYAN *see* RIAN

SADBH, SABHBH *m & f*

Is considered to mean 'sweet' or 'goodly'; it was the name of several well-known legendary women, one of whom, the daughter of Conn Cétchathach (Conn of the Hundred Battles), according to a tale in *The Colloquy of the Ancients*, headed the list of the four 'best women in Ireland who ever lay with a man'. She was wife of Ailill Olom, a legendary Munster king, who was accused of raping Áine, the love-goddess. They had three sons, Eoghan, Cian and Cormac, and a foster-son, Lughaid, who was nursed on the same knee and at the same breast as Sadb's own son Eoghan. Sadbh Sulbair (Sadbh of the pleasant speech) was a daughter of Ailill and Medb, queen of Connacht, who led the men of Ireland against the Ulstermen in the *Táin Bó Cuailnge*. A possible English form is *Sive*.

SAOIRSE *m & f*

An Irish word meaning 'freedom' or 'liberty' which has been adopted as a personal name, mainly, if not exclusively, for women. There is no recognised English form, indeed, almost by definition, such a concept would be ludicrous.

SÉAFRAID, SÉAFRA, SÉATHRÚN m

Irish forms of the name *Geoffrey*, introduced to Ireland by the Anglo-Normans. One of the most renowned bearers of the name was Séathrún Ceitinn (Geoffrey Keating), the historian and poet. Born in Co. Tipperary *c.* 1570 he was educated for the priesthood at an Irish college in Bordeaux. He returned to Ireland as a curate about 1610, becoming renowned for his sermons. His interest in Irish history led him to write his most famous work *Foras Feasa ar Eirinn* (History of Ireland), in the compilation of which he toured the country, consulting books and manuscripts. His surviving poetry includes religious pieces and laments for dead friends. He died about 1650 and is buried at Tubrid, Co. Tipperary. The English form is *Geoffrey*.

SÉAMUS, SÉAMAS *m*

A name borrowed, mainly through English, from the New Testament Latin name *Jacobus*. It was common among the Anglo-Norman settlers, as in the case of James, Earl of Desmond, who is habitually described as Séamus Iarla Deasmuman (James Earl of Desmond) in Irish sources. A more recent bearer of the name was Séamus Murphy, the Cork sculptor and stone-carver, who was born near Mallow in 1907. As his reputation grew he was commissioned to create busts of prominent people; in Áras an Uachtaráin are bronze busts by him of all the Presidents from Douglas Hyde to Cearbhall Ó Dálaigh. He died in Cork in 1975. The English form is, of course, *James*.

SEÁN, SEAAN *m*

This is the form of the Latin *Joannes* borrowed through Norman French. It was used, for example, in 1248, as *Seoan Puitiler*, of John Butler when he went plundering along with Jordan de Exeter; it fairly rapidly, like other imported names, came into use among the Irish, as with Seán son of Pilib (John son of Philip), son of Giolla Íosa Ruadh Ó Raighilligh, king of Muinntear Mhaoli Mhordha — 'an excellent, prosperous, wealthy man' who died, prematurely, of disease, in 1401. A recent bearer of the name was Seán Lemass, born in Dublin in 1899, who after serving in the Rising of 1916 and opting for the Republican side in the Civil War, became a TD in 1925 and, as a founder-member of Fianna Fáil, was appointed Minister for Industry and Commerce in de Valera's first government in 1932. He was elected Taoiseach in 1959, from which office he resigned in 1966 and died, in Dublin, in 1971. The English form of the name is, of course, *John*. 'English' forms such as *Shaun* or *Shawn* should be avoided, though *Shane* on analogy with surname forms like *McShane* is acceptable, as should 'feminine' forms such as *Shauna*.

SEANAN, SENAN *m*

A diminutive form from *sen*, *sean* (old, ancient). There were quite a number of saints who bore this name, of whom Seanan of Inis

107

Cathaig, Co. Clare, is the best known. He was born at Kilrush, Co. Clare, in the sixth century; one evening as he was guarding his father's cattle on the sea-shore a mighty wave broke unexpectedly by his feet, but then the tide ebbed so that he was able to make his way dry-shod across the bay; immediately he had done so the waters closed in again. He regarded this as a sign that he was to take up the religious life: he broke his weapon in two and made a Cross of it. After studying at Kilnamanagh, near Tallaght, in Co. Dublin, he travelled the country before returning home to establish his monastery on Inis Cathaig in the Shannon estuary. After evicting a ferocious monster that inhabited the island (by making the Sign of the Cross in front of it), he observed that the sea could, on occasion, become wild and tempestuous, making passage to or from the island extremely hazardous; he arranged with the angel who was accompanying him that safe passage would always be afforded his monks. Possibly as a result of this arrangement pebbles from the island are believed to give protection from destruction by shipwreck. Seanan's Feast Day is March 8th; the best English form is *Senan*.

SENAN *see* SEANAN

SHEENA *see* SÍNE

SHEILA *see* SÍLE

SÍLE f
Is a borrowing of the Latin *Cecilia*, or its abbreviated form *Celia*, a name given prominence by St Cecilia, details of whose life have been romanticised. The name was brought to Ireland by the Franks; it became especially popular in the later medieval period. In 1471 Síle, daughter of Niall Garv O'Donnell and wife of Niall, the son of Art O'Neill, was in Omagh castle with a body of troops in the absence of her husband when it was besieged

and subsequently captured by Henry O'Neill. The best form in English is *Sheila*.

SÍNE f

A variant form found in Co. Derry of the name *Sinéad*, itself a diminutive form of the French *Jehane, Jeanne*, the equivalent of *Jeanette*. Its proper English form should be simply *Jane*, but it may have been the source of the increasingly popular *Sheena*.

SINÉAD f

A diminutive form of the French name *Jehanne, Jeanne* or *Jeannette*, introduced to Ireland by the Franks or Anglo-Normans. It has recently become very popular. One of its outstanding bearers in modern times was Sinéad Flanagan, born at Balbriggan, Co. Dublin, in 1878. Her career was in teaching and in her spare time she taught Irish for the Gaelic League. She was also interested in amateur dramatics and, indeed, at one time considered the stage as a career. One of her Gaelic League pupils was Éamon de Valera, a teacher of mathematics, later to become heavily involved in Irish politics and eventually to become President of Ireland, whom she married in 1910. She wrote fairly extensively for children — plays, poems and fairy-stories. She died in 1975. The literal English equivalent of the name is, of course, *Janet*, though *Jane* is often used.

SIOBHÁN, SIBÁN f

This is a borrowing from the French *Jehanne, Jeanne*, the feminine form of *Jean* (John), brought into Ireland by the Franks or Anglo-Normans in the twelfth century. A notable modern bearer of the name was Siobhán Mc Kenna, who was born in Belfast in 1923, from where she moved with her family to Galway at the age of five. She was educated in Galway and acted in the Taibhdhearc, the Irish-language theatre in Galway, before joining the Abbey Theatre in Dublin in 1944. She enjoyed great success on the stage, in film and on television. Among her notable triumphs were the title-role in Shaw's *Saint John* and Pegeen Mike in Synge's *Playboy of the Western World*. Among the eight films in which she appeared was *Doctor Zhivago*, in 1965. She was declared 'Actress of the Year' in 1958. She died in Dublin on November 16th, 1986. The only English form of the name is *Joan*.

SIVE *see* SADBH

SOMHAIRLE *m*
This is a name borrowed from an Old Norse name meaning 'summer-farer' or 'summer wanderer' which was particularly popular among the Mac Donnells of Antrim. One of its best known bearers was Somhairle Bui Mac Donnell, who was born about 1505. He was imprisoned in Dublin Castle from 1551 to 1552 and on his release seized the constable of Carrickfergus and exacted a heavy ransom. In 1575 he was defeated at Toome by Essex. His wife and family, whom he had sent to Rathlin Island for safety's sake, were victims of the extirpation of the entire population of the island by Sir John Norris in 1575, with Francis Drake as the naval commander, while 'Sorley Boy' watched helplessly from the mainland. He died in 1590 and is buried at Dunineany Castle. The received English form is *Sorley*.

SORCHA *f*
This name means 'bright' or 'radiant'. It is another example of a name which was popular in the Middle Ages, went into a slight decline and then was restored to recent popularity. It has been equated with *Sarah* or *Sally*, but of course it has no connection with either. The best form, in Irish or English contexts, is simply *Sorcha*.

SORLEY *see* SOMHAIRLE

SUIBNE, SUIBHNE *m*
A name thought by some to mean 'well-going'. It was born by several saints and by a High King. The best remembered Suibhne, however, is Suibhne Gelt, a king in Dal Araidhe. On the eve of

the battle of Magh Rath, in which St Rónán attempted to conciliate between the two antagonists, the saint displeased him by marking out the site of a church in his territory. The displeasure increased at Rónán's intervention in the hostilities — and Suibhne killed one of Rónán's choristers, and even attempted to kill the saint. Rónán cursed him, and his descendants, and Suibhne, driven mad by the curse, was forced to fly through Ireland, suffering many miseries, until, eventually, he went to the church of St Moling, where he died. The usual English form is *Sweeney*.

SWEENEY *see* SUIBHNE

TADG, TADC *m*

This name literally means 'poet' and despite its use by kings, such as Tadc mac Cathail, a king of Connacht who died in 1023, and of several saints, it is particularly appropriate that it should have been borne by Tadg Dall Ó hUiginn, one of the greatest of the later bardic poets. He was born in 1550 in Co. Sligo and fostered, apparently, in Co. Donegal. Only about forty of his poems survive — mainly addressed to his patrons — the Maguires, O'Neills, O'Rourkes and O'Connors. In the North of Ireland the name was generally anglicised, *Taig* or *Teague*, which are used as abusive terms for Catholics or native Irish.

TAILLTE, TAILLTIU *f*

In Irish legend she is the daughter of mac ú Moir and gave her name to Mag Taillten, in Co. Meath, where the celebrated assembly known as Aonach Taillteann was held at the beginning of August. The place is a prehistoric cemetery and games in honour of the dead were a primary function of the assembly. To preside at the assembly was a prerogative of the king of Tara. The last assembly was held in 1168 under the presidency of Ruaidhrí O'Connor of Connacht, who thereby asserted his claim to the High Kingship. The place is now known as Teltown, overlooking a loop in the River Blackwater. A relic of the ancient assembly is considered to have consisted in the 'Teltown Marriages', which survived until the eighteenth or nineteenth century; these were celebrated in a ring-fort known as Rathdoo or Ráth Dubh; a couple could be wed there and, if they failed to agree, could return there, stand back-to-back in the middle of the fort, and, by walking, one to the north, the other to the south, thereby dissolve their marriage. There is no real English form.

TAIRDELBACH, TOIRDHEALBHACH *m*

With the meaning 'abettor' or 'instigator' this was a name borne by a number of kings, including Tairdelbach úa Conchobair, king of Connacht and of Ireland, who died in 1156. One well-known bearer of it was Toirdhealbach Ó Cearbhalláin (Turlough Ó Carolan), the best known of Irish harpers and composers, who was born in Co. Meath in 1670. At the age of fourteen he was blinded by smallpox and was apprenticed to a harper. His first piece is considered to be 'Sí Beag is Sí Mór' a song about two fairy hills (actually Passage Tombs) in Co. Leitrim; his last was 'Slán le Ceol' (Farewell to music), composed just before his death in 1732. In between were many pieces written for landlord patrons, and, of course, his celebrated 'Concerto'. The best form in English is *Turlough*.

TARA *see* TEMAIR

TEAGUE *see* TADG

TEMAIR, TEAMHAIR f

The meaning is probably that of *teamair* (eminence, elevated place); at first sight the use of the English form *Tara*, as a female personal name, appears an affectation — using the place-name of *Teamhair* (Tara, Co. Meath). But according to one piece of *Dinnseanchas* (place-name lore) it was after a lady called *Teamhair* that the royal site in Co. Meath was named. Therefore by a curious sort of reflux the use of the English form of the place-name, *Tara*, as a female personal name, *Tara*, unexpectedly appears respectable.

TERESA *see* TREASA

THOMAS *see* TOMÁS

TIARNA(CH) *see* TIGERNACH

TIARNÁN *see* TIGERNÁN

TIGERNACH, TIGHEARNACH, TIARNACH m

From *tigern* (lord); several saints bore this name. The best known was probably Tigernach of Clones, Co. Monaghan. In his youth he had the misfortune to be captured by Welsh pirates and taken to Britain; he managed to escape and make his way to the celebrated monastery of Candida Casa, at Whithorn in Galloway, in Scotland. Here he received his education for the priesthood and from here he went on pilgrimage to Rome. In Rome he is said to have acquired relics of the apostles Peter and Paul, which he brought back with him to Ireland, where he founded a monastery at Clones. He was renowned for raising the dead to life — one of whom was no less a person than Duach, Bishop of Armagh. He died at Clones in 549; his Feast Day is April 4th. The best English version of his name is *Tiarnach* or *Tiarna*.

TIGERNÁN, TIGHEARNÁN, TIARNÁN *m*
Another name derived from *tigern* (lord); it was borne by at least one saint and, naturally enough, by chieftains, princes and kings. The best known bearer of the name is probably Tigernán Úa Ruairc, king of Breifne, who at first opposed the ambitions of Turlough O'Connor, king of Connacht, but was soon forced to submit and enter into an alliance with him, only to defect in 1132; by 1138 he had rejoined O'Connor in alliance and in 1142 was rewarded with a share of the eastern half of Meath. On being deprived of this in 1144 Tigernán changed sides again, only to be forced to submit to Muirchertach Mac Lochlainn, king of Cenél Eogain, a fresh contender for the High Kingship of Ireland, in 1149. By 1152 Úa Ruairc had made himself so obnoxious and untrustworthy to so many people that he was deprived not only of his fortress at Dangan, but of his recently acquired territorial gains. He also lost his wife, Dervorguilla, to Diarmaid Mac Murrough. Eventually his career ended in his assassination at the hands of the Franks or Anglo-Normans in 1172. The most viable anglicisation of the name is *Tiarnan*.

TOMÁS *m*
This is a borrowing of the biblical name *Thomas*. Before the Anglo-Norman invasion the name was used only by clerics, such as

Tomás, a bishop and scribe and abbot of Linn-Duachail, who died in 807. It was 'reintroduced' by the Normans, amongst whom it was fairly widely used: Tomás mac Muiris Mic Gearalt died in 1213, while Tomás son of Seán Dalton died in 1393 and also in 1393 Tomás Mortimer arrived in Ireland. In recent times the name was borne by Tomás Ó Criomhthain, the celebrated author of An tOileanach (The Islandman), born on the great Blasket off the Kerry coast in 1856. The book describes the hardships and isolation of island life, written, as Ó Criomthainn says, because 'there will not be our likes again'. He died, on the island, in 1937. The English form is, of course, *Thomas*.

TREASA f

It has been suggested that this name means 'strength'. It has been used as an Irish equivalent of *Teresa*, for St Teresa of Avila and, more recently, for Thérèse of Lisieux; it has, of course, no connection with these imported names. *Treasa* is the best form in Irish or English.

TRÍONA see CAITRÍONA

TURLOUGH *see* TAIRDELBACH

UILLIAM, LIAM *m*

This is a borrowed form of the Old German name *Willahelm*; it was brought to England by the Normans and thence to Ireland. It was, of course, common among the Anglo-Norman families such as the de Burgos, and patronymic versions — *Mac Uilliam* — developed fairly quickly. It was adopted reasonably quickly by some Irish families. In 1381, for example, Uilliam son of Donagh Muimneach O'Kelly, Lord of Hy-Many, 'a man of the greatest character, worth and renown of his own tribe; the man who had given a general invitation of hospitality to the schools of Ireland [i.e. Brehons, poets, historians, harpers etc] and had given them all their demands, died a very old man, after the victory of penance' — despite his foreign fore-name he maintained a native tradition. The curtailed form, *Liam*, is the form currently in use in Ireland. The English form is, of course, *William*.

ULTÁN *m*

Meaning, simply, *an Ulsterman*, it was the name of a score or so of saints. The best known, and the most loved, was Ultan (Ultán moccu Conchobair) of Ardbraccan, Co. Meath, where he became abbot and bishop of a monastery founded by St Braccán. He had a reputation for austerity: he used to bathe regularly in cold water regardless of the weather — possibly it is in commemoration of this that another name for the monastery was *Tiobraid Ultáin* (Ultan's Well). His particular devotion was to children, of whom, indeed, he is more or less the Irish patron saint. He is said to have 'fed with his own hands every child in Erin who had no support'. He provided particular care for the children of women who were carried off by the plague. In addition to his charitable works he achieved a considerable reputation for scholarship: a skilful and elaborate poem, 'Brigit bé', in honour of St Brigit, as well as a *Life* of Brigit and a Latin poem in her honour have been attributed to him. Tírechán, the biographer of St Patrick, was a disciple of his. He died at

Ardbraccan between 656 and 663. His Feast Day is September 4th; the English version of his name is, simply, *Ultan*.

ÚNA f

Úna was the legendary mother of Conn Cétchathach (Conn of the Hundred Battles) and the name was also used of the *bean sídhe* of the O'Carrolls. In later medieval Ireland it was a popular name, as with Úna, daughter of Tadg, son of Manus O'Conor and wife of Maguire, who died in 1395, or with the Countess of the County of Clare, Úna, daughter of Turlough, son of Murtough, son of Domnall, son of Tadg, son of Turlough, and wife of the Earl of Thomond, who died in 1589. Its best known bearer is probably she who is remembered in *Úna Bhán* (Fair Úna). Tomás Láidir Costello, a late seventeenth-century poet, had fallen in love with Úna, a girl much richer than he; her parents disapproved and Úna fell into a wasting sickness; Tomás was invited to visit, Úna showed signs of recovery. Tomás left so as not to compromise her by staying in her room. He hoped to be called back but made a foolish vow to wait no longer than half an hour before crossing a stream on the way home. The summons came after he had crossed the stream. Because of his vow he refused to return. Úna died and was buried on an island in Lough Key; Tomás swam out to the island on three successive nights, mourning Úna in the words of the song. The name is sometimes anglicised *Oonagh*.

W

WILLIAM *see* UILLIAM